D1568247

MY OFF-SEASON WITH
THE DENVER
BRONCOS

MY OFF-SEASON WITH

THE DENVER BRONCOS

BUILDING A CHAMPIONSHIP TEAM (WHILE NOBODY'S WATCHING)

LOREN LANDOW
WITH MIKE KLIS

TAYLOR TRADE PUBLISHING
Lanham • New York • Boulder • Toronto • Plymouth, UK

Authors' note: The fitness advice in the following chapters is not intended to take the place of your doctor's or personal trainer's recommendations. Consult with your trainer or physician about any changes you wish to make after reading this book.

Published by Taylor Trade Publishing
An imprint of The Rowman & Littlefield Publishing Group, Inc.
4501 Forbes Boulevard, Suite 200, Lanham, Maryland 20706
www.rowman.com

10 Thornbury Road, Plymouth PL6 7PP, United Kingdom

Distributed by National Book Network

British Library Cataloguing in Publication Information Available

Library of Congress Cataloging-in-Publication Data Available

ISBN 978-1-58979-751-2 (cloth : alk. paper)
ISBN 978-1-58979-752-9 (electronic)

∞™ The paper used in this publication meets the minimum requirements of American National Standard for Information Sciences—Permanence of Paper for Printed Library Materials, ANSI/NISO Z39.48-1992.

Printed in the United States of America

Contents

Acknowledgments

To my wife, Becky, and my friends at Golden (Highway 93) Starbucks whose encouragement and black coffee refills made this book possible. *—Mike Klis*

Thank you to Michelle, Taylor, and Morgan for being my drive and inspiration, while allowing me to give fully to those I coach—I love you guys more than I could ever show. Thank you to my mom, Loretta, and stepdad, Don, for showing me love, strength, determination, and self-accountability. To my brother, Bill, and sisters Kalen and Jen for showing me unconditional love, strength, and support. Thank you to all of my aunts, uncles, and cousins for support through the years; family is everything! Thank you Mike and Mary Marlene and all of the Nevins for their support and love. Thank you to my mentors in no particular order: Loren Seagrave, Greg Roskopf, Steven Plisk, Tom Purvis, Jim Warren, Paul Godinez, Mike Allen, Kathy Barrett, George Solich, and Rich Andrews. To those who have left my life way too early: Uncle Guy Maggio, Mark McKee, and Jason Vigil, you are in my daily thoughts, and I am continually motivated to be the best I can knowing you are helping me along my way. Thank you to my childhood friends Drew Ostrem, Shawn Brooks, Ryan Rego, and Shane Haas; your friendship and support didn't go without notice. Thank you to all of my athletes over the years, no matter how old, young, elite, or novice, you all inspire me to be better and have helped shape me to be a better coach and person. Without you all,

I am nothing. I am so honored, humbled, and blessed to be your coach! Thank you to Mike Klis, editor Amy Rinehart, and publisher Rick Rinehart for putting up with me during this process! Thank you to my interns of the summer of 2011, Ashleigh Floyd, Christa Poremba, and Isaiah Castilleja. Thank you Kathleen Courier for capturing great photos. Judianne Atencio, thank you for all that you do! And to anybody I have failed to mention, it was not intentional, you are all special to me. Last but not least, thank you Brian Dawkins and Chris Kuper for trusting me to work with you and the players. What a special opportunity! —Loren Landow

Building a Championship Team While Nobody's Watching

TIM TEBOW just threw perfectly to his target from 25 yards away. Demaryius Thomas caught the pass in stride as he was running a shallow post pattern and finished off the 80-yard catch-and-run touchdown that gave the Broncos their upset play-off victory against the mighty Pittsburgh Steelers.

Everywhere there was bedlam.

A crowd of 75,000-plus shook the structure that was Sports Authority Field at Mile High. Tebow sprinted the length of the field in exaltation, thanking the Lord, cheering the play, and then, not knowing what else to do, jumped into the south end zone for his first-ever Mile High Leap.

Bar patrons across the Rocky Mountain region were heard chanting, "Te-bow! Te-bow!" Apartment building balconies were filled with people screaming with joy.

Denver was delirious. Meanwhile, the man who helped start it all was at home in his living room watching on TV with his family.

Loren Landow, who had watched the first half on a Frontier flight that was bringing him back from a coaches' conference in San Antonio, jumped so high off his couch, he could have touched the ceiling. His eight-year-old daughter, Taylor, jumped and jumped and jumped. His wife, Michelle, jumped so excitedly, the Landows' five-year-old daughter, Morgan, fell off her lap.

Morgan got over it.

Landow rejoiced for Tebow, rejoiced for center J. D. Walton, felt so happy for the likes of left guard Zane Beadles, middle line-backer Joe Mays, punter Britton Colquitt, running back Lance Ball, receiver Matt Willis, defensive lineman Robert Ayers, and Mr. Tackle-Eligible Chris Clark, to name a few.

Forgive Landow if he felt a warm measure of satisfaction. These were his guys. He would never say this, of course.

Landow is the director of sports performance for the renowned Steadman Hawkins Clinic. He is not only known from improving an athlete's speed and agility; he does not shirk the importance of team building. For so many Broncos players, Landow was the only coach they knew during the off-season when the NFL lockout barred them from their team headquarters and the coaches who were employed within.

Now, as he watched the Broncos celebrate their play-off win on TV, Landow, a quiet, humble sort, did not say Tebow or the other Broncos were *his* athletes. It didn't even cross his mind.

As a guy who works personally with Tebow twice a week, Landow knows that no elite athlete, much less one who has achieved the highest honors in football, can attain such success without dozens of people helping along the way. Hillary Clinton had it right. It does take a village.

Still, Landow remembers the first time he watched Tebow train with several other Broncos during an organized, players-only workout in the midst of the NFL lockout in the spring of 2011.

"My first impression was he would run through a wall for you,"

Landow said. "But he didn't have great body control and didn't yet know how to use his body like a rhythmic, well-oiled machine."

Later, when the lockout was settled and the Broncos were a couple of weeks into training camp, Landow got a call from Tebow. The quarterback wanted one-on-one workouts during the regular season.

Tebow and Landow talked. Landow doesn't begin any training session without an opening conversation to find out something about where his new client thinks he is now, and where he hopes to finish. Not that athletic performance is ever finished. While going over goals with his latest new client, Landow used the term "bull in a china shop" to describe Tebow to Tebow himself.

"Yeah," Tebow told Landow, "but a bull in a china shop is hard to tackle sometimes."

The Broncos had not been to the play-offs in six years. They were playing the Steelers, who had been to the Super Bowl three times in six years, winning two. Not surprisingly, the Steelers were heavily favored against the Broncos in a first-round AFC play-off game on January 8, 2012. Although the Broncos were playing at home, they were 8½-point underdogs.

And yet, at the end of regulation, the Broncos and Steelers were tied, 23–23. Tebow, who had been in a late-season swoon that had emboldened his many critics, had rebounded and was playing well against the Steelers, throwing for one touchdown and running for another.

Overtime began with a coin toss, which the Steelers called and lost. Russ Hochstein, another offensive lineman who had worked with Landow during the lockout, motioned to the referee that his Broncos would receive the ball first.

Hochstein was filling in for injured right guard Chris Kuper, who as a starter since early in the 2007 season was the Broncos' offensive lineman with the greatest seniority. It was Kuper who first gathered so many of his offensive line mates to Landow's workouts during the lockout. The offensive line workouts with

Landow led to team captain Brian Dawkins organizing players-only team workouts with Landow.

The players-only workouts became known as Camp Dawkins. The veteran safety, who went on to earn his ninth Pro Bowl berth by season's end, financed the workouts. Paid the rent for the facilities. Paid Landow's fee. Paid for the lunches, fruit, and water that Judianne Atencio brought to every workout. Atencio had arranged for the group to get hydrated by Eldorado Spring Water, and the local Powerade team backed up their van every few weeks and dropped off cases of the product.

"The best thing about this is, we're together as a team," Dawkins said after the first session on May 10. "It's a bunch of guys that want to work. It's a time of year where a lot of what you enjoy is being around your teammates."

Atencio runs ProLink Sports, a public relations and marketing firm. She does publicity work for Landow and Dawkins. Atencio can't get enough credit for serving as the bridge that enabled so many Broncos players to train properly—dare we say, train more efficiently than any other off-season regiment?—while so many other NFL teams and players were left to fend for themselves.

"As a competitor, you'll always be able to give a little bit more if you have somebody with a whistle pushing you," said Rod Smith, the retired, all-time leading Broncos receiver who stopped by to watch the Dawkins-led second workout at the South Suburban Sports Dome in Centennial. "How many guys you know are throwing 25-pound medicine balls right now? Nobody. Except these guys."

It was those Camp Dawkins off-season workouts during the lockout—where Landow essentially served as the only coach to Broncos players—in the solitude of various sports facilities in the Denver area that became the seeds to the Broncos' surprise play-off run in 2011.

Kuper helped plant those seeds. Unfortunately, his injury in the final game of the regular season—a gruesome ankle dislocation

Joe Mays, holding a medicine ball, rests between overhead medicine-ball throws for explosive power.

in which his foot was almost completely turned backward—would not allow Kuper to enjoy the fruits of playing in his first postseason game.

Football can be a cruel game. Which is why victories are so sweet, and play-off wins so treasured.

With the NFL's relatively new overtime play-off rules, the Steelers' offense would get an offensive possession unless the Broncos unexpectedly scored a touchdown on their first drive.

Unexpected, because the Broncos had not scored a touchdown since there were 10 minutes and 36 seconds left in the second quarter.

But as Tebow jogged onto the field for the first play of over-time, he could take comfort in knowing he had prepared for moments like this.

Some of that preparation was Tebow's remarkable string of magical final-quarter comebacks that led to the AFC West title and the right to play the Steelers in this first-round play-off game. Final quarter? In most cases, Broncos' wins did not come until the final minutes, even seconds.

The Broncos were 1–4 when Tebow replaced Kyle Orton after five games. Put that 1–4 record after the Broncos' 4–12 mark in 2010, and there wasn't much optimism flowing through Dove Valley.

Spirits didn't improve as the Broncos were down 15–0 late in game six, Tebow's first start of the season, against the Dolphins in Miami. But then Tebow stunningly, almost mystically, let it rip. He threw two touchdown passes in the final 2:44 and ran in a game-tying, 2-point conversion to stunningly send the game into overtime, whereupon a 52-yard field goal by Matt Prater won it.

The magic of Tebow had cast its first spell.

Tebow also rallied the Broncos from a 10-point deficit late in the third quarter to defeat Oakland. He was down 13–10 with less than two minutes remaining in back-to-back games against the New York Jets and San Diego Chargers. The Broncos won them both.

In the Chargers' win, Tebow carried the ball for an NFL quarterback record twenty-two times. Afterward, he said he felt not beat up, or sore, but remarkably fresh. Landow took some satisfaction in that.

Against the Minnesota Vikings, Tebow and the Broncos had just one first down by halftime. They scored 28 points in the second half, including a short Prater field goal with two seconds left to prevail, 35–32.

Against the Chicago Bears, Tebow was 3 of 16 passing through three quarters, and the Broncos were down 10–0 with less than 2:15 remaining. Tebow threw a touchdown pass and directed the offense to a game-tying field goal, albeit a 59-yarder by Prater with eight seconds left in regulation. Prater connected again in overtime, this time from 51 yards out.

In most of those comeback victories, when the games reached their do or lose moments, that's when the Broncos would do.

"When you get Tim to a position where he can ad-lib, the thought process goes out the window, and he can go off natural recall," Landow said. "He is such a natural athlete, and I think that is why he is so successful out of the pocket, and his on-the-field instincts are truly amazing."

Tebow had a 7–1 record through eight starts and was the most popular player not just in the NFL, but on the planet. Sure, some luck went his way. But Tebow's hard work and preparation allowed him to seize good fortune when it fell his way.

Well before he started pulling off the confidence-building, miraculous rescues, Tebow's preparation began on May 19, when Tebow joined Camp Dawkins.

Admittedly, Tebow joined the Dawkins-Landow workouts only because he was getting grief for not attending during the first week and a half.

"Tell Tim Tebow we're looking for him," LenDale White, a

Broncos running back, said after the second team session with Landow.

White was smiling as he poked fun at the Broncos' star. The local media had been critical of Tebow for not working out with his teammates when it appeared he did have time to make commercials for Jockey undergarments and to make national appearances to promote his autobiography, *Through My Eyes*.

In this case, perception was not reality. Tebow was working out every day, a couple of hours a day, wherever he was. Weights, cardiovascular conditioning, taking snaps from under center, dropping back and throwing to receivers he picked up wherever he was.

The truth is, Tebow didn't train with the Dawkins group because he trusted his own workout. He didn't know anything about this Landow guy.

"I'm not a guy that at all will be trusting, especially when you're dealing with my body," Tebow said. "And when the team started working out with him, I was as hesitant as anybody, because I'm not going to let someone hurt me or affect my body in a bad way."

The negative public perception, though, did cause Tebow to surrender. He did start showing up at the Dawkins-Landow workouts for two or three days at a time, then taking off to attend a charity event or golf tournament or ESPY Award show for a week or so. Then he'd come back for a few more days of training with the team.

Ironically, by season's end, Tebow would become one of Landow's most regular and loyal clients.

"Just through time he definitely earned my trust with him as a trainer and as a friend, too," Tebow said. "He's good at what he does."

No one works out harder than Tebow. No one. He was doing four-hundred push-ups and four-hundred sit-ups a day when he was eleven years old. During his two training camps with the

Broncos, Tebow won every post-practice conditioning sprint. Not most of them. All of them.

As a rookie in 2010, he would follow coach Josh McDaniels's grueling two-a-day training camp sessions by working out on his own for another hour.

In the midst of all the dedicated work ethic, though, Landow saw flaws in the movement patterns of most of the participants.

"The athlete should move in an orchestrated and fluid manner," Landow said. "Most of the patterns I saw Tim and the other athletes working with were inhibited [in] those manners."

Meaning what, exactly?

"Roughly describing it, they almost try too hard," Landow said. "Two reflexes that are paramount to athleticism; first, the cross-extensor reflex, and second, the stretch-shortening reflex. The cross-extensor is a normal pattern of opposing limbs that allows for fluid locomotion; when athletes get tense and try to run harder, this reflex can be disrupted, and the patterning becomes less natural and rhythmic. The stretch-shortening reflex is described as a relaxed muscle; when stretched, [it] has greater potential to generate high force; when it is shortened, to create more power into the ground when we sprint, change direction, and jump. If an athlete learns how to run relaxed, both reflexes can be optimized, yielding a quicker, faster, and more explosive athlete. To optimize both reflexes, there are multiple skipping and sprint coordination drills that can be implemented in the warm-up, and during the actual movement sessions."

Tebow walked into the South Suburban Sports Dome—otherwise known as the bubble to Broncos players, who practice there during inclement days in the regular season—on May 19 wearing blue Nike shorts, a T-shirt, and cleats. Camp Dawkins would not start for another hour, but Tebow wanted to throw to receiver Britt Davis and tight end Dan Gronkowski and take snaps from Walton.

"This is an opportunity to gain ground on, not necessarily teams, but players, because it's an opportunity to get better," Tebow told the *Denver Post* prior to his session. "This part is more important to show that we're all together. I know a lot of us have been throwing and catching and doing what we need to do other places, but I think this is big, just to show that we're together. You can come together a few times to show, 'Hey, we've got each other's backs.'"

Still, Tebow was somewhat shamed into attending. Kyle Orton, the Broncos' starting quarterback until further notice, had attended Landow's early workouts. Tebow and another Broncos quarterback, Brady Quinn, would attend later.

In fact, in the second half of the Broncos' player workouts, Quinn had stepped up to become the camp's leader. By the end, it was really Camp Quinn more than it was Camp Dawkins, as the safety kept to his regular routine of spending the latter part of June and the first half of July with family.

Interestingly—if not all that surprising to those familiar with the tension between the Broncos' quarterback group—Orton, Tebow, and Quinn never worked out at the same Landow-directed session. One of the three was almost always there. But never two at the same time.

Landow never worked with the quarterbacks during their pre- and post-workout throwing sessions. But Landow's client list, which began in 1999 when he started training center Todd McClure, punter Brian Moorman, and defensive end Aaron Smith—all of whom were still playing in the league through the 2011 season—for the NFL combine, is more than three hundred NFL players long.

Landow knows an NFL player when he sees one. When developing an athlete, Landow takes a full-spectrum approach. Developing athletic bio-motor abilities specific to the sport is key. When talking about football, the bio-motor abilities are speed, power, agility, strength, neuromuscular coordination, flexibility (mobility and stability), and energy-system development (sports-specific conditioning). Landow takes quality over quantity with Tim Tebow, just as he does with all his athletes.

Whether it is sprinting or throwing mechanics, the force needed for each originates from the same place: the ground. In throwing, the inside edge of the rear foot anchors into the ground to initiate the chain reaction to the knee, hip, core, and, finally, through the arm. In sprinting acceleration, driving the foot behind the hips propels the body forward. The stronger the athlete is from the foot/ankle, knee, hips, core/torso, and upper extremity, the more force the athlete can put into the ground, yielding greater speed. For efficient transfer of ground reaction forces, the core must be stable and strong. In many athletes, core training is busy work and lacks transfer ("crunches"). The lumbar-pelvic complex needs to have great stability in order to generate and absorb force, keeping the athlete healthy while maximizing his performance.

Stability Series and Core Exercises

Plank (beginner). Alignment from ear to ankle. Weight distributions forearm and ball of foot. Arms parallel. Core braced, avoid low back collapse. Hold until technique is compromised.

Plank with hip hike (intermediate). Alignment from ear to ankle. Weight distributions forearm and ball of foot. Slow tempo; raise the hips without shifting weight from the forearms. Slow tempo; lower the hips back down to the start position. Hold and repeat until technique is compromised.

Plank with leg raise (advanced). Alignment from ear to ankle. Weight distributions forearm and ball of foot. Slow tempo; raise one leg 3–5" without losing stability in low back. Slow tempo; lower leg back to the floor and repeat on the same leg until technique is compromised. Repeat on other side.

Lateral plank elevated on 6–8" box with leg lift (advanced). Alignment from ear to ankle. Elbow under shoulder and perpendicular to torso. Weight distribution on forearm and feet. Brace through core, shoulder girdle, hip, and ankle. Lift top leg with lateral hip and hold until technique is compromised.

Lateral Stability

Lateral plank kneeling (beginner). Alignment ear to knee. Elbow under shoulder and perpendicular to torso. Weight distribution on forearm and knee. Brace through core, shoulder girdle, and hip. Hold until technique is compromised.

Lateral plank (beginner). Alignment from ear to ankle. Elbow under shoulder and perpendicular to torso. Weight distribution on forearm and feet. Brace through core, shoulder girdle, hip, and ankle. Hold until technique is compromised.

Lateral plank elevated on 6–8" box (intermediate). Alignment from ear to ankle. Elbow under shoulder and perpendicular to torso. Weight distribution on forearm and feet. Brace through core, shoulder girdle, hip, and ankle. Hold until technique is compromised.

Posterior Stability

Posterior hip lift (beginner). Seated L position with hands behind hips. Weight distribution on hands and heels. Push into the ground with the hands and the heels to lift the hips. Extend hips to achieve alignment from ear through ankle. Brace core and shoulder girdle, hips, and dorsi-flex feet. Slowly lower and repeat until technique is compromised.

Posterior plank (intermediate). Seated L position with hands behind hips. Weight distribution on hands and heels. Push into the ground with the hands and the heels to lift hips. Extend hips to achieve alignment from ear through ankle. Brace through core, shoulder girdle, hips, and dorsi-flex feet. Hold position until technique is compromised.

Posterior plank with leg raise (advanced). Seated L position with hands behind hips. Weight distribution on hands and heels. Push into the ground with the hands and heels to lift the hips to extension. While holding the plank, slowly lift one leg 3–5" off ground while maintaining level hips. Slowly lower leg back to ground and repeat until technique is compromised.

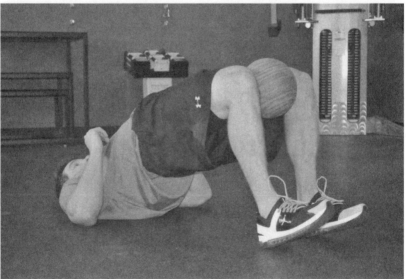

Posterior activation (adduction). Lying supine with knees bent at 90 degrees, feet dorsi-flexed. Squeeze ball between knees and push through the heels to extend the hips while bracing the core. Slowly lower back to the ground while maintaining the squeeze on the ball while bracing the core. 6–8 repetitions.

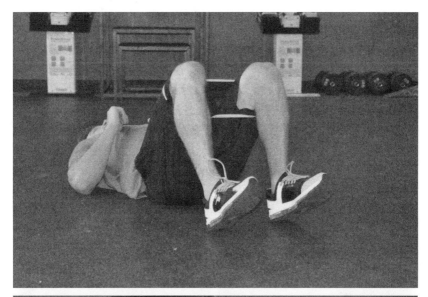

Posterior activation (abduction). Lying supine with knees bent at 90 degrees, feet dorsi-flexed. Push out into band and push through the heels to extend the hips while bracing the core. Slowly lower back to the ground while maintaining a lateral push on the band while bracing the core. 6–8 repetitions.

Anti-rotational Exercises

Seated alternate leg raise (beginner). Seated on box with 90-degree angle of knee joint. Arms across chest, back flat, core braced. Slowly lift one foot off the ground 3–5". Slowly return the foot to the ground and alternate legs without shifting the hips or losing stability in the core. Repeat for 30–45 seconds or until technique is compromised.

Seated partner rhythmic stability (intermediate). Seated on box with 90-degree angle of knee joint. Arms across chest, back flat, core braced, and feet flat pushing into ground. Partner applies a push/pull force, and the exerciser must resist motion. Force is directly related to the ability of the exerciser. Continue for 20–30 seconds.

Standing partner anti-rotation stability (advanced). Squat position with arms extended holding a physioball. Feet straight with heels flat and pressure on ball of foot. Squeeze ball and have partner push in varying directions. Exerciser resists the effort of the partner for 20–30 seconds.

Kneeling cable chop (advanced). Kneeling with a split stance, cable set while grabbing the rope with two overhand grips. Full extension in the spine, lift and rotate the cable across the torso with slight shoulder rotation while avoiding any movement in the hips. Slowly lower the rope back to the starting position. 6–8 repetitions or until technique is compromised.

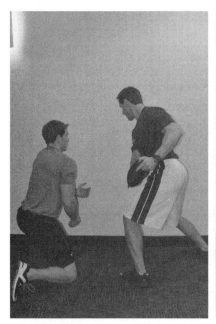

Sandbell power rotations (advanced). Staggered athletic stance. Rotate back while holding medicine ball or sandbell. Push feet into ground to initiate the movement and push through the legs and rotate through hips and shoulder to maximize the rotational velocity. 5–8 repetitions.

Throughout training sessions with the quarterbacks (Tebow and Brady), the transfer of forces would be reiterated. Whether it was an offensive lineman needing a burst of acceleration to reach the second level, or a defensive back closing the distance on a receiver, the hows and whys of maximizing the body's ability to be efficient would be reinforced each training session.

Thomas, a second-year receiver who was selected with the number 22 overall pick, three spots ahead of Tebow, in the first round of the Broncos' 2010 draft, was split a few yards to the left. Assigned to cover Thomas was the Steelers' best defensive back, Ike Taylor.

As Tebow barked the cadence from the shotgun, Steelers' free safety Ryan Mundy scooted up from his deep coverage spot to near the line of scrimmage on Thomas's side.

Incredulously, at that point the Steelers had no one deep in coverage. All eleven defenders were within a few yards of the line of scrimmage, or "box" in football parlance.

Tebow took the shotgun snap from Walton. There was nothing sophisticated about the play call. Only two guys went out—Eddie Royal, lined up on the right, ran a simple buttonhook; Thomas, on the left, cut diagonally toward where Mundy had originally been positioned.

It's a pass play that's not difficult to defend—provided there are enough people back to defend. That wasn't the case with the Steelers' defense on this play. Since Tebow had become their quarterback halfway through their fifth game, the Broncos had led the NFL in first-down rushing plays. The Steelers were ganging up to stop the run on the first play of overtime.

That was why the simple pass call by offensive coordinator Mike McCoy worked so beautifully. Royal attracted three defenders, including the Steelers' other safety, All-Pro Troy Polamalu.

Mundy wasn't back to help Taylor, whom Thomas immediately beat off the line of scrimmage.

Tebow saw Thomas had a step in the clear and zinged a pass that hit Thomas head high at about the 38-yard line. Thomas ran, then stiff-armed Taylor a few yards behind him.

Thomas was off, sprinting down the right sideline in front of the Broncos' bench. The stadium was filled with people jumping to their feet. "Go! Go! Go!"

Mundy had recovered in time to track down Thomas, but the Broncos receiver outran the angle. Thomas ran through the end zone, which was so slick that he slid and shuffled until he ran halfway up the field's exit tunnel.

The Steelers would not get an offensive possession. The touchdown, on the first play of overtime, took just 11 exhilarating seconds. The Broncos had won a play-off game. Tebow had just thrown a beauty.

"It was such a quick throw," Landow said. "There was no need to look off. It was right to him. Tim was already in the right position. It was a quick drop, and he loaded up and let it fly."

CHAPTER 2

The Lockout

N NFL WORK STOPPAGE figured to hurt the Broncos more than any other team. They had a brand-new guy running their front office in John Elway. They had a brand-new head coach in John Fox.

And they had no idea who would become their starting quarterback.

Actually, that's not completely true. Elway, Fox, and general manager Brian Xanders had a pretty good idea that within hours after the lockout ended, whenever that would be, they would appease Kyle Orton's trade request, and Tim Tebow would become their quarterback in 2011.

Elway had been officially hired on January 6 as the Broncos' new executive vice president of football operations. Orton was in his office the next day essentially saying he was too established as a starting NFL quarterback to take a backseat to Tebowmania.

And so the plan was to trade Orton and give their 2010 first-round draft pick a shot, provided that Tebow could beat out Brady Quinn in training camp and the preseason, which the Broncos hierarchy hoped would be the case.

And if Tebow was going to be the quarterback, it was clear he would need all the training he could get.

On so many levels, the Broncos needed an off-season of work. And they needed that work as individuals coming together as a team, not a team of individual players.

Each year, the NFL off-season begins around March 1. This is when unrestricted free agents can typically begin negotiating with other teams, and teams can make trades.

Players under contract typically are called to begin team conditioning between March 15 and 30.

But one of the league's most contentious labor disputes in years changed all those starting dates for the 2011 season. The dispute between owners and the players' union was mostly about money, of course. The players wanted status quo. They were getting roughly 59.5 percent of the revenues—not including $1 billion the owners took off the top for "enhancing-the-game" funding such as stadium improvements and the NFL Network.

The total revenues were $9.3 billion in 2010, so the players were getting 59.5 percent of roughly $8.3 billion.

The owners said that because the status quo left them with dangerously thin profit margins and would not allow them to grow their booming business, the players needed to give back a couple of percentage points of the game's revenues. Make that a lot of percentage points. The owners wanted to drop the players' cut of the $8.3 billion to around 50 percent, a hefty giveback considering the pooh-bahs already got the first $1 billion.

The difference was gaping enough to fear the labor lockout would last into the regular season. Not even the most cynical person thought the league would cancel the 2011 season—as Major League Baseball did in 1994.

But a significant delay appeared inevitable.

The start of the 2011 league off-season was first set at March 11—later than normal in an attempt to give the two sides extra negotiating time. Then the start date became March 18.

And then, the owners went forward with their lockout, which put the 2011 NFL season on hold until further notice.

Both sides aired their complaints publicly, with each side saying the other was unreasonable. For the most part, the fans didn't care. The media portrayed this as billionaires squabbling with millionaires. Only a handful of the thirty-two owners might have been billionaires. And far less than half of the players were millionaires.

But it only took a couple of each to dramatize an otherwise dull story.

For all but a small fraction of the players, the lockout meant they were not permitted to show up at their respective team's facility. They had been informed of the labor issues but didn't want to cram their minds with information they couldn't control. Broncos player reps Brian Dawkins, Kyle Orton, and Russ Hochstein could worry about the particulars.

Just tell us when to show up, was the attitude of most players.

Which wasn't in March, April, May, or June. Or most of July.

Not only could players not visit their team headquarters: They could not interact with coaches, who were placed on the management side of the labor dispute. They could not get in shape or lift weights with their team strength and conditioning coaches. They could not participate in Organized Team Activity (OTA) practices or minicamps.

The players were on their own.

Brian Dawkins may have been blessed with the quick-twitch muscles of an elite athlete, but physical twitch should not be confused with mental impulse.

Dawkins is nothing if not deliberate. As a 37-year-old safety who, labor situation willing, would be entering his sixteenth NFL season, he well knows how NFL players are preyed upon. NFL players have money. Even a rookie playing on a minimum salary will make $390,000 in 2012. And NFL players aren't always careful

Dawkins hydrates after some high-tempo agility drills.

with their money. Given a choice, they'd spend $80,000 to restore a car rather than build a savings account, much less a retirement fund. Then again, name a twenty-something male who is careful with his money, however much he has.

NFL players run into people with nice clothes, warm smiles, firm handshakes, and generous natures who tell them: Invest in this; buy that. All it takes is for a player to get burned once—a car that leaks, a house that creaks, an investment policy that tanks— and he becomes distrusting for life. At least he should.

So when Judianne Atencio approached Dawkins with Loren Landow's proposal in early April, the veteran player was hesitant but intrigued. "Why did you put this proposal together?" Dawkins asked. "Someone had to," Atencio said. "And I have a way to help you do it."

Building a Championship Team While Nobody Is Watching

In light of the current lockout in the NFL, huge ground can either be gained or lost during the early months of the off-season.

Whether it is speed and power development, general off-season conditioning, or team camaraderie, losing time in the off-season can be detrimental to success. Without a structured plan moving forward, many veterans are enjoying the "extra" time down before off-season workouts and OTA's. The downside to the time down will be the potential injury rash that may hit players when the first OTA begins from not having a consistent and structured plan.

Loren Landow is the Director of Sports Performance for Steadman Hawkins. Over the past 15 years Coach Landow has trained over 400 Pro Athletes for the NFL combine, NFL off-season, MLB, Oympians, NHL, and NBA. Coach Landow's philosophy is simple: make athletes as fast and explosive while reducing their likelihood of injury. Coach Landow has been sought after as a consultant for many orthopedic specialists and professional organizations to implement his training strategies for success.

The plan is simple. Start getting players prepared for the demands of the season. The training will consist of Movement (speed and agility), Resistance (strength, plyometric), Energy System Development (conditioning that is based on the demands of the position played). A four-day per week training that is split into two sessions per day. All sessions will be overseen and coached by Loren and his assistant coaches. There will be two separate times that players can choose to train, either 9:30 a.m. or 11 a.m. We will utilize the sports dome in Centennial, Colorado, for our movement sessions as well as more football related activities if the lockout should continue into early summer. The goal would be to run more position-specific groups from the interior line play to the perimeter game.

Monday Movement: Group 1) 9:30 a.m. Group 2) 11 a.m.
Monday Strength: Group 1) 11:30 a.m. Group 2) 1 p.m.
Tuesday Movement: Group 1) 9:30 a.m. Group 2) 11 a.m.

Tuesday Strength: Group 1) 11:30 a.m. Group 2) 1 p.m.
Wednesday: OFF or Make up session
Thursday Movement: Group 1) 9:30 a.m. Group 2) 11 a.m.
Thursday Strength: Group 1) 11 a.m. Group 2) 1 p.m.
Friday Movement: Group 1) 9:30 a.m. Group 2) 11 a.m.
Friday Strength: Group 1) 9:30 a.m. Group 2) 1 p.m.

Times may change due to group size. The goal is to keep athlete groups to no more than 15. If participation is greater we will add other times. I can be reached for further discussion on program and training at 000-000-0000.

Landow was working out many of the Broncos players as individuals. His most regular clients were offensive linemen Chris Kuper, J. D. Walton, and Zane Beadles. Ryan Harris and Tyler Polumbus, former Broncos offensive linemen, were also part of Landow's group.

Atencio, public relations expert that she is, thought it was important for Broncos fans to know that lockout or no lockout, the team's players were working on getting in shape. Between Landow and Dawkins, two people for whom she coordinated marketing and publicity, why not bring them together for team-organized workouts?

Thing is, Landow was thinking the same thing. So was Dawkins.

"I knew I wanted to do something but didn't know how to go about it," Dawkins said.

Dawkins continued to monitor the labor battle. No, that's not right. It's not right to say he was monitoring the situation. He was *involved* in the labor talks. For Dawkins was more than a player representative. He was also a long-standing member of the Players Association's executive committee. And the labor dispute was hung up in courts for five weeks while he deliberated whether to go forward with team-organized workouts.

"Yes, I thought it through because this was a decision that was about more than just me," Dawkins would say later in the days leading up to the Super Bowl XLVI game between the New York Giants and New England Patriots. "I care about the guys who would be working out. You're talking about safety and wanted to make sure nobody got injured. Wanted to make sure everybody had a little something to eat afterwards. All those things."

The two parties, owners and players, had not been engaging in any meaningful negotiations. A couple of big court rulings were coming up, one in St. Louis, which would appeal the judgment in Minneapolis, but to wait on the court system to decide on one's fate is to wait. And wait.

The media, with little else to report on, hammered on the presumption that when the lockout did end, players would be rushed into an abbreviated training camp and season.

These players would be out of shape. At best, the play in 2011 would be sloppy—although many prognosticators believed the labor dispute would cause a delay in the season, no one thought the two parties would be silly enough to wipe out a season in a league that had been generating an estimated $9.3 billion in annual revenues.

At worst, teams would suffer devastating injuries.

"People were talking about how players would be out of shape, because there would be no OTAs, no minicamps," Landow said. "As I looked at it, I saw a convergence of acute and chronic injuries, based on not having enough workload in off-season."

Most of the Broncos players were working out in various groups across the country. But if they all pulled together as a team, Broncos fans would be encouraged. Plus, Landow believed many players would be working out incorrectly. Landow was confident enough in his own coaching ability to handle a situation like this. A situation of uncertainty. A situation of trepidation. Yes, a situation where players were fearful of the unknown.

Players would never admit to this, but they want to be led. They want discipline. They are comfortable when their day is by rote.

Landow, kneeling, talks to Dawkins about the training objective for the day.

Landow and Atencio thought Dawkins was the only Broncos player with enough panache to pull the players together for an organized workout.

Ordinarily, the starting quarterback is by nature the face of the franchise. The Indianapolis Colts were Peyton Manning. The New England Patriots are foremost Tom Brady's team. Think San Diego Chargers, and you think first of Philip Rivers.

The quarterback is the leader of almost every successful franchise. The exception may be the Baltimore Ravens and middle linebacker Ray Lewis. But even the rugged, physical, defensive-oriented teams such as the Pittsburgh Steelers and New York Giants would consider quarterbacks Ben Roethlisberger and Eli Manning, respectively, to be their most irreplaceable players.

The Broncos' quarterback situation, though, was a different story. Orton was the starting quarterback, but it wasn't his place to bring the guys together in the off-season, because everyone knew that as soon as the lockout ended, he would go on the trading block.

Tebow couldn't assume leadership of the team until Orton was out of the way. Same with Brady Quinn.

Take away the quarterback position, and who was the Broncos' true captain?

It was a no-brainer. Dawkins is one of the top leaders of the NFL, perhaps right behind the great Ray Lewis. There wasn't much question that the only Broncos player who could bring other Broncos players together was Dawkins.

"I had a strong feeling that this would not have happened had I not done it to the level we did," Dawkins said. "Again with me, I wanted to win this year. I wanted guys to have a safe haven in order to get in shape and get ready. I knew from being in labor meetings and negotiations that there was a potential that this thing had a chance to drag out. There was so much up in the air. So for as long as I could, I wanted to keep things as familiar as it usually is for us. And still be able to keep a flexible enough schedule so they can go off and enjoy their off-season, too. One thing I wanted to make clear is there wasn't going to be any kind of punishment if guys couldn't come. I know people took count of who was there and who wasn't there. I didn't care. All I cared about is if you didn't have a place to go, you now had a place to come and work out with the guys, to get some footwork in and help the Broncos win."

Drew Brees beat everybody to it. Not that there was a competition on who could put together the first team-organized workout or who could conduct the best team-organized workouts during the lockout.

But if there were, Brees would have been named the league's off-season MVP. Remember the point about how the starting quarterback is usually every team's go-to guy?

Brees was the star quarterback of the New Orleans Saints who, amid much fanfare, conducted the first team workout during the lockout on May 3.

What made the event a national story was, first, the sizable media covering the first workout; and, second, an impressive thirty-seven players showing up for the first day. Considering the Saints only had fifty-three players on their active roster when their 2010 season ended, a 70 percent attendance spoke to the power Brees had with his teammates.

Brees took weeks to organize the organized workouts. It was impressive that he secured Tulane University's indoor athletic facility. He paid some of the Tulane football staff to run some drills and brought in his personal trainer, Todd Durkin, from his days with the San Diego Chargers.

The Saints didn't just condition: they ran plays. It was almost as if they were running their own minicamp. Just without the supervision of head coach Sean Payton and his coaching staff.

Dawkins, meanwhile, still wasn't quite ready to say "go" on the Broncos' organized workouts.

"We're not like the Saints," Dawkins said on May 6. "That's a veteran team with a quarterback and head coach who have been together for a while. Those guys know their playbook. They can run their plays, because they've been running those plays for five years.

"It's not like that with us."

The Broncos players didn't know their playbook, because for the most part, they didn't even know their head coach. At least, not formally. John Fox was hired in January, as the Broncos players had begun their off-season vacations in various parts of the country.

The league had pretty much told each team their coaches were not to have contact with the players until a new collective bargaining agreement was reached.

There was a 24-hour window, which coincided with the first

round of the 2011 draft on April 28, when a Minnesota judge lifted
the lockout. A federal appeals court in St. Louis stayed the Minnesota judge's decision—meaning the lockout was back on—as the
NFL was conducting its second round on April 29.

During that 24-hour window, though, Fox did get out his new
playbook to his players. He had some pick them up at the facility
and he overnighted the playbooks to those who were out of town.

Still, a playbook can be nothing more than lines and diagrams
drawn on a paper if there isn't a coach around to show the players
how to execute the plays. A day after getting out his playbooks, Fox
again had no players to coach.

"If we do get together," Dawkins said on May 6, "we won't be
running plays or scrimmaging against each other or anything like
that. We'll just be getting together to break a sweat, get in shape,
build some camaraderie, things of that nature."

As he spoke, Dawkins was close to making the call. He had
multiple phone conversations with Landow. He attended one of
the Landow-run workouts attended by several of the Broncos players. By the night of Friday, May 6, Dawkins was satisfied Landow
was just the man to lead the Broncos through their off-season
conditioning program.

On the weekend of May 7–8, Dawkins started sending out texts
and e-mails to his teammates. An eight-time Pro Bowler at the time,
Dawkins let his friends know that if anyone cared to work out
together as a Broncos team, they would meet three or four times a
week at the bubble, starting Tuesday.

No pressure. Don't make last-minute travel arrangements if
you're out of town. It will just be there if you want it. Some guy
named Loren Landow would be the one leading the workouts.

CHAPTER 3

The Performance Coach

BRIAN DAWKINS would not commit to Loren Landow until he saw the performance coach's work. With his own eyes.

"Had to," Dawkins said. "Talked to him in person. Talked to him on the phone. Asked him what he had the guys do on some of his hard days."

Dawkins was struggling to not only turn over his body and well-being to a guy he didn't know, but his teammates' bodies as well. Nothing personal against Landow. He could have been the greatest performance coach in the United States. (In fact, many of his clients say he is.) It's just that Dawkins didn't know him.

It's hard to trust what you don't know.

Who is Loren Landow?

He didn't know himself during his freshman year at the University of Northern Colorado (UNC). Growing up in Westminster, and skating by at Westminster High School, Landow picked UNC for the noblest of reasons.

"I got in?" he said, smiling. "I wasn't a great student in high school."

He changed that in college. Located about sixty-five miles northeast of downtown Denver in the half-college, half-rural town of Greeley—where the smell from the meatpacking farms can be strong and the nightlife weak—Northern Colorado brought out the serious student in Landow.

He started pulling good grades as a freshman but still was undecided about his field of study until he took a career-path course that one day gave its students a 600-question questionnaire.

The results: Loren needed to be a teacher of athletics.

"I felt that was a very weird result," he said. "Did that mean a coach?"

Soon thereafter, he realized his field would be exercise physiology.

"I do think working out was a passion of mine," he said.

Maybe because as a child he had spent much of his time lying in a hospital bed, having the strength to work out or play games seemed little more than a dream. A dream Loren never surrendered. But a dream the local hospital receptionists and nurses might have thought was unrealistic as they got to know Loren on a first-name basis.

"I think sometimes with children, maybe males more than females, they will do a lot of denial," said Loretta Cawelti, Loren's mom. "So even though he knew he had limits, there were things he could do. But I wasn't surprised because his whole time as an adolescent, in high school, it was all athletics."

In many ways, Loren Landow was a precocious child. He developed a strong work ethic and unusually strong understanding of accountability from his stepfather, Don Cawelti. He developed an uncommon sense of purpose from his strong, driven mother, Loretta.

Loren had big, blue eyes and pale blond hair. He had dreams, ambition. He was a competitive kid who had his share of childhood success as a three-sport athlete.

For all his positive characteristics and qualities, Landow had just one problem: Breathing.

From the time he was nine months old until shortly after his ninth birthday, Loren's asthmatic condition periodically delivered unwanted visits to hospitals.

One time he stayed eight days, and much of that was in intensive care. Other trips were for a couple days. Many were overnight stays to stabilize his condition.

"It stopped him from a lot of physical activity that other kids could do," Loretta said. "He couldn't play basketball or soccer or football."

Yet, despite his condition, Loren was a star on the playground during recess—mom didn't have to know everything! And he was a natural on the ski slopes. The cold air, his parents would come to find out, was good for his lungs.

"At five we took him up for a half a day at Winter Park and we took him up a practice hill," Loretta said. "And there he went down the hill backwards. I'm trying to ski to catch him, but he went all the way around and down this hill backwards. I mean, he loved it."

For reasons not easily explained, Loren eventually reached a point where he could function normally despite his asthma.

"A lot of Loren's asthma was environmental issues," Loretta said. "Trees and sometimes just the air, pollution. A lot of his asthma was exacerbated by the pollen in the spring. It's a seasonal issue. It's a strange disease.

"If there was a flu bug going around, he'd have it. And then it'd be asthma for him. A sudden change in the weather. It was interesting: skiing never seemed to bother him."

Loren was not yet two years old when his parents divorced. Loretta remarried when Loren was four.

Don Cawelti was a renaissance man who would become a major influence in Loren's life.

Don once built a plane and flew it. He once built a car and drove it. He built homes and lived in them.

"In a single-engine plane we left Denver, we went through Mexico," Loretta said over lunch in mid-February. "Down to Latin America. We crossed South America; we went up to the Caribbean and back to Florida. And then back to Denver. That was one trip. We only did it once. That was enough. That's the kind of thing he would do. I was just a bystander who held my breath a lot."

She laughed at the memory. And, no, Loren and the other kids did not join their parents on this single-engine excursion through the southern hemisphere.

"I don't think anyone was too pleased about us taking that trip," Loretta said. "Nothing was beyond [Don]. When the kids went to bungee jump, he went and bungee jumped. And I mean, he was not a youngster at that time."

As a corporate attorney for Public Service Company of Colorado and Denver's National Western Stock Show, Don Cawelti once argued a case before the U.S. Supreme Court. He won that case on appeal.

"You would never say to him, 'I can't do that,'" Loren said. "He always held himself to high-level accountability. I never heard him blame anybody for something he did. I learned that through him. Today with my work, I hold myself accountable to these athletes."

Exactly what does it mean to say Don held himself and others to a high level of accountability?

"It meant he didn't take a lot of BS," Loretta said.

Maybe, because as a trial lawyer, Don knew BS when he heard it.

"He kind of challenged the kids—Loren, in particular, being the youngest," Loretta said. "If you didn't like school—'Hey, it's the only game in town.' There was nothing they could say that could be used as an excuse; Loren remembers countless occasions when his brother Bill and he would brag after a long day of skiing how they never fell. Don would quickly respond, 'That means you weren't trying hard enough.'"

Don usually got home around 6 p.m. He and Loretta believed in a family dinner. Steve, Don's oldest son, was already out of the house by then. But there were usually four kids under one roof—Jenny, who was Don's oldest daughter; and then Loretta's children: Kalen, Bill, and Loren.

"And they were all kind of achievers," Loretta said. "Consequently, for Loren, there was a lot of competition. Competition colored him a great deal."

"Where's South Dakota?" Don would ask.

"Of course, Loren was young; he never knew the answer," Loretta said. "Loren is still trying to win dinnertime with his own family. Don would say if the train was coming from Colorado Springs at sixty miles an hour, and another train is going south from Denver, where would they meet? And the older ones would have the kind of skills to figure it out. There was always a competition in our family."

By now, it should be obvious Loretta was not exactly a submissive wallflower. Although her education didn't go beyond high school, she is extremely smart and in recent years has not exactly lived the retirement life. To the contrary, she has been a longtime executive director at two synagogues, first at Temple Sinai and now at BMH-BJ.

As executive director, she is in charge of all secular matters related to the building, the grounds, the hiring and firing, the finances.

She speaks fondly of Don and her children, and with a certain amount of detachment that is rare among mothers.

"Get in the car," Loretta once told her son during Loren's sophomore year in high school.

Loren was stunned. "What for?"

"Just get in the car," Loretta said.

She drove until she pulled into a Sylvan Learning Center parking lot.

Loren knew the jig was up. He had horrible grades in school. True, with the meds that were poured into his body for much of his youth, it was a wonder he could focus at all. But the Landows and Caweltis were an intelligent, achieving family.

Steve was a stockbroker. Kalen has been in the publishing business all her life. Bill is a director in technical communications. Jenny is a paralegal.

And Loren was pulling down Cs, Ds, and the occasional F. From ages twelve to fourteen, Loretta put Loren in tae kwon do. Only she doesn't call it that.

"I always say karate was the most important thing for a child like Loren," she said. "It made him focused. It made him disciplined. It taught good sportsmanship. I believe in it. I always tell parents who might have a discipline situation with their children, I tell them: 'Get them in karate.' I think it was life-changing for him."

Except as a high school underclassman, and long after he stopped competing in tae kwon do, Loren was still a bad student. And so now mom had made the surprise trip to Sylvan.

"We get into the Sylvan parking lot," Loren said, "and before she says anything, I tell her, 'No, mom, I'm not dumb. I'm just lazy.'"

Quite the admission for a high school junior. They kept their appointment with Sylvan but never went back. Loren Landow would never again slough off in classes and never had a grade below a B after that trip to Sylvan.

Eventually, Loren filled out physically and became a decent, three-sport high school athlete. His classmates, though, remember him most as a competitive bodybuilder.

"My uncle Guy, when I was fourteen, he bought me my first weight set," Landow said.

The 98-pound weakling was ready to follow his dream. Through weight lifting Loren got bigger and stronger, and through size and strength came confidence.

He had two friends who also liked to lift weights—Sean Brooks and Jason Vigil. Sean and Jason went from weight lifting to dabbling in bodybuilding.

Loren followed his friends and, from ages seventeen to twenty-one, became a local, state, and national competitor in the drug-free, bodybuilding sanction.

In 1991, when Loren was eighteen, he won the Teenage Colorado contest.

Some bodybuilders are especially strong in the legs. Others feature their biceps. Still others have chests and shoulders that would shame the Greek gods.

"I was symmetrical," Loren said. "There was not one thing that stood out."

It was from bodybuilding that Landow learned the most extreme form of discipline. Not the kind of discipline necessary for getting a B+ in the classroom, or the type of discipline millions of people across the world need to show up for work on time.

To have his body ready for pose and flex on competition day, Loren followed a strict diet. For five years, Loren lived on dry tuna fish (no bread), rice, and egg whites. He'd eat tuna four or five times a day.

"I can't eat tuna now," he said. "Can't go near the stuff."

The key to looking good, Landow says now, is about intake. You can work out all you want. But nutrition is equally important. It's a combination of working out and the dietary intake.

This was the type of discipline required of a champion competitor. Which requires not just discipline but extreme sacrifice.

It was while preparing for one of his final bodybuilding competitions that Loren received a crushing blast of perspective. Tragically, Jason Vigil, his bodybuilding partner and one of his best childhood buddies, took his own life.

Loren was devastated. But it also steeled him. He used Jason's death to make himself even more determined, more disciplined in his training.

Said Landow about this difficult period in his life: "When one of my best friends died while I was training for the contest, it was at that point I decided that our days are numbered. If you are going to do something in this lifetime, you better make it count!"

To this day, one of Landow's most repeated training mottos is: Train to win!

And, he added, "To win, one must believe they are worthy to do so. The final result in competition won't always be a victory or a gold medal, but the will to prepare as though it is separates the champions versus the rest of the field! This holds true for every occupation. There are three things one must do to win: one, out-work your competitor; two, outsmart your competitor; three, intimidate your competition.

"If you complete one and two, number three takes care of itself!"

Following his junior year at UNC, Landow decided to retire from bodybuilding so he could concentrate on his studies in exercise physiology. But a degree is one thing. Degrees can branch into several careers. Which occupational branch would Loren follow?

"I didn't want to come out of school to be a personal trainer," Landow said. "I figured cardiac rehab was a great way to go."

He did have an influential professor in Dr. Jackson. She taught the EKG classes that Landow enjoyed in college.

"When you work with heart attack patients, it's not unlike working with athletes, in that you're helping to change quality of life, change daily habits," he said.

Fresh out of college, he got his first job at South Denver Cardiac Rehabilitation Clinic. For six months, Loren would rehab cardiac patients. He mostly worked with older clientele. The pay was poor, and the stress level was high.

Stress? One time, Loren was leading a man in his twenties

through a stress test when the guy went into cardiac arrest. The guy made it, but Loren was shaken.

He decided cardiac rehab, while one of life's most noble pursuits, wasn't for him. He couldn't see going through it the rest of his life.

Landow moved on to become a personal trainer with the Colorado Athletic Club on Monaco Parkway.

"I worked there six months when I met a gentleman who became my first mentor," Landow said.

At one time, Jim Warren was known as Barry Bonds's personal trainer. This was in the early to mid-1990s when the ultimate measure of baseball greatness was 40-40: 40 stolen bases and 40 home runs in the same season. A rare feat of speed and strength.

But in 1998, Mark McGwire and Sammy Sosa captivated a nation with their chase of baseball's long-standing home run record. Roger Maris hit 61 homers in 1961, which broke Babe Ruth's record of 60 homers set in 1927.

McGwire and Sosa became the biggest sports story in ages. McGwire would finish with 70 homers, and Sosa had 66. Later, allegations that McGwire and Sosa were steroid users would tarnish their remarkable home run chase.

But well before McGwire and Sosa had fallen, Bonds decided that for the 1999 season, his goal would no longer be 40-40. That was so two years ago. His new goal would be 71 home runs.

That resulted in a different form of training. Warren decided to end his relationship with Bonds.

"I learned a lot from Jim," Landow said. "I shadowed him. On and off for a year-plus. He was an unbelievable motivator. I learned about consistency. In this business, you have to deal with guys who aren't responsible. Guys would blow it off. They'd be late."

To combat such apathy, Landow would consistently tell his athletes: "Don't sacrifice what you want most for what you want at the moment."

Landow would further explain: "You may want ten more minutes of sleep, but will that take away from your goal of making the Pro Bowl? Another contract? A starting job?" If someone showed up a little late, he'd admonish him with: "Somebody was enjoying their pillow more than success."

Landow is big on motivational quotes. And as he continued his work as a personal trainer at Club Monaco, as it was frequently called by its members, he knew that eventually he wanted something more than working with the weekend athlete or the wife who wanted to lose fifteen pounds.

Not that Loren considered himself above the common American fighting the bulge. To this day, people will meet Loren for the first time, find out what he does for a living, and ask him for some quick advice. And Loren will always graciously comply.

It's just that Loren had attained enough expertise in the field of exercise physiology that he was ready to offer his skills to the serious athlete. The dedicated athlete with goals of grandeur, whether that be Olympic gold or playing in the big leagues.

"But I didn't want to jump into it too early, because I knew you would only have one shot at this," Loren said. "I wanted to make sure I knew what I was doing and was on top of this from the day I got started with the elite athlete. Because if you don't do it right with one athlete, you're done. It's a word-of-mouth business."

During his time at Club Monaco, Landow read countless volumes of text and research.

"Every night after work—I would say, my first eight years of work—I would read three hours a night books and research related to my profession," he said.

Such discipline. Such commitment. Where did he get it?

"Bodybuilding," Landow said.

After his time with the Colorado Athletic Club on Monaco, Landow moved on to the Inverness Colorado Athletic Club where he stayed for another eight years. It was at Inverness where Landow began to dip into training the serious athlete. These days, serious athletes start well before they become men and women. They start when they are still boys and girls with fundamental training.

Landow "started doing guinea pig work with the middle school and high school athlete. I was always afraid to get too busy too soon with pro athletes."

This led to a job in late-1998 at the Pro Line Management in Englewood, where he started combine training for NFL hopefuls. Sessions were held both at the Inverness health club and the South Suburban Sports Dome.

Through local sports agents Peter Schaffer (All Pro Sports and Entertainment) and Robb Nelson (Proline Management), Landow got his first three NFL combine clients: center Todd McClure, punter Brian Moorman, and defensive end Aaron Smith.

All three were still in the NFL through the 2011 season: McClure with Atlanta, Moorman with Buffalo, and Smith with Pittsburgh.

Landow had found his niche.

Looking back, Landow admits that in the late-1990s he was not much different than other performance coaches, the few of them that there were.

"I was always working on my craft, doing research on techniques," Landow said. "But it's fair to say that, looking back, I wasn't fully polished in my teaching methods. It was more about burn calories, work hard, run more, lift more. It was football. I'm much better at understanding the sciences of my craft now. Performance training is still about how your methodologies complement your philosophies."

Landow's philosophy? He has a simple explanation: "Make athletes efficient."

The execution of that philosophy is a sophisticated mix of biomechanics, human physiology, anatomy, and biochemistry.

See, Tim Tebow doesn't really know his body. No athlete knows his body like Loren Landow does. Most athletes just know when they feel good, feel lethargic, feel fast, feel slow, feel strong, feel weak.

Even if Landow didn't know then what he knows now, his clients swore by him. Even if his techniques weren't yet advanced, Landow was a keen motivator. He had the knack of pushing his athletes but in a likable manner.

His business spread by word of mouth. He went from the Inverness Colorado Athletic Club to Velocity Sports Performance in 2003, where he started training Broncos defensive end Trevor Pryce, center Tom Nalen, linebacker Bill Romanowski, and former University of Colorado standout linebacker Chad Brown, who went on to have a terrific career with the Pittsburgh Steelers, Seattle Seahawks, and New England Patriots.

These players helped Landow gain the reputation of getting more mileage out of those who were nearing the end of their careers.

New athletes would sign up, but more telling about Landow were his repeat customers. He did football camps for Anthony Munoz, a Hall of Fame left tackle; and Jerry Wampfler, the former Colorado State head coach who was an NFL offensive line coach from 1973 to 1993.

Landow's philosophical messages played well at camps, where impressionable youth would hang on every word.

"Loren was concerned with the whole person," said his sister Kalen. "Not just their body. He was concerned that they not do destructive things outside of football. He looked at the bigger picture. Kids who were always late, kids who were not coachable—from Loren's viewpoint, what good was training if you were like this?"

"And not because of me," Landow said. "I tell these guys: This is who you are. Whether you buy my BS or not, do what the coach or your boss tells you. I come across great athletes all the time who don't make it because they're not coachable. There's a trickle-down effect with the rest of the team. Coaches can't have that. Bill Belichick will get rid of a Randy Moss to sign a Danny Woodhead.

"It's a system, it's a philosophy. You're trying to instill something that's bigger than athleticism."

When Jason Vigil died, Landow was crushed. He dealt with the grief of his passing through workouts and training.

"Not a day goes by that I don't think of him, and that was seventeen years ago," Landow said. "But I believe that in difficult times and tragedy we can have one of two outcomes. One, let the circumstance or situation consume us. Or, two, we can persevere and overcome the struggles and become stronger for it!"

It all started with Chris Kuper, Zane Beadles, and J. D. Walton at the Big Bear Ice Arena in the Lowry subdivision. They are the middle of the Broncos' offensive line. Kuper is the right guard; Walton, the center; Beadles, the left guard.

It was late February 2011. The text messages between players, the buzz among the NFL front offices, the talk on SportsCenter was that the labor lockout would shut down the league's off-season at least. Maybe some of the regular season.

That didn't mean the players had to shut down. Kuper had been working out with Landow for three years. He recruited Beadles and Walton to come work out with his trainer.

By mid-March, Landow's group had moved from Big Bear to Sports Xcel, a facility that was closer to the Broncos' headquarters, but still oh, so far away.

The labor lockout engaged. Instead of organized full-team workouts at the Broncos' headquarters—where there's soft green grass, a state-of-the-art weight room, and comfortable locker rooms—Kuper, Beadles, Walton, and right tackle Ryan Harris had been gathering individually at Sports Xcel, a warehouse structure in Englewood with far more quality athletic training than space.

Dawkins was among the majority of players who were working out elsewhere. He already knew how to get his body ready.

The lockout lingered. As the team's primary player rep, Dawkins knew a labor settlement wasn't close. Getting the boys together for some sweat and laughs would be sweet.

But in 2011, there was now an almost saturated market of performance coaches. What set Loren Landow apart? Dawkins eventually settled on reputation.

"Coming from where he came from—director at Steadman Hawkins—that makes him established," Dawkins said. "That says a lot. That name for me spoke volumes, that they trusted him to run their particular program."

During his time working at Inverness and then Velocity, Landow worked with athletes who were also clients of Mike Allen, the director of physical therapy at the Steadman Hawkins Clinic in the south Denver suburb of Greenwood Village. The clinic specializes in orthopedic care. Landow and Allen would send players back and forth between them, depending on need.

Chad Brown and Bo Scaife, the former Mullen High School star and Tennessee Titans tight end, were among the Allen-Landow group.

As Velocity was about to close its doors in 2008, Allen invited Landow to become director of sports performance at Steadman Hawkins, easily the most renowned clinic for surgeons and physicians in the nation, never mind Denver. On April 5, 2011, Landow sent Dawkins a proposal titled "Building a Championship Team While Nobody Is Watching."

A paragraph from this proposal details his recommendations for the program:

> The plan is simple. Start getting players prepared for the demands of the season. The training will consist of Movement (speed and agility), Resistance (strength, plyometric), Energy System Development (conditioning that is based on the demands of the position played). A four-day per week training that is split into two sessions per day. All sessions will be overseen and coached by Loren and his assistant coaches. There will be two separate times that players can choose to train, either 9:30 a.m. or 11:00 a.m. We will utilize the sports dome in Centennial, Colorado, for our

movement sessions as well as more football related activities if the lockout should continue into early summer. The goal would be to run more position-specific groups from the interior line play to the perimeter game.

"Then once I talked to him, once I saw what they were doing," Dawkins said, "I saw that he was doing things that I was already doing. All those things came into play.

"I thought about it and then met with him and went out to see what he was doing with his workouts." Landow vividly remembers one thing Dawkins told him that day: "He told me, 'We need to be doing this.'"

Later, Dawkins added: "I talked to some of the guys who worked with him and prayed about it and I felt led that this was the right direction to go. He was a guy who was going to work guys hard, but at the same time he wasn't going to beat them up

Dawkins and the group prepare the body with dynamic flexibility "inch worms."

and not allow them to recover. That was the biggest thing for me. I wanted to work hard while you're there and still have the ability to recover and enjoy your off-season."

The lockout was on. The Broncos had their performance coach. And make no mistake, Landow wanted to coach the Broncos through this time of uneasy uncertainty.

Remember how mom said competition colored Loren greatly? Well, Landow, as a lifelong Broncos fan, didn't want to see his team fail in 2011 because the players weren't working out properly. He could help. He wanted to help. And now he had Dawk's blessing.

It was time for Landow to go to work on the Broncos.

The Broncos' First Team Workout

RONCOS PLAYERS weren't quite sure what to expect when they gathered around sports performance coach Loren Landow for the first team-organized workout. But Landow knew exactly what he would deliver:

My philosophy for sports training is quite simple—prepare the human body for the demands for the sport.

This means from a metabolic demand, a biomechanical needs, and a coordinative perspective, my exercise selection must have transfer in one or all of these aspects for effective transfer and a best use of training time.

The human body is a highly adaptable organism to training stress. The SAID principle is a training theory that essentially states, "What I train for, I get."

Of course, if it were really that easy anyone could do this job. In training, the goal is to find exercises that have transfer. However, because the body adapts so well, there is a need for variation. Coaches who pepper the athlete with the same stress over and over again, the body adapts (which is a good thing), but too much of the same thing leads to accommodation; and the body will not only plateau but, even worse, start to downslide from the previous state of training.

A good coach knows when, why, and how to change the variables. Not unlike a good play caller, once the opposition is starting to notice a pattern or trend, a good coordinator knows this is the time to throw a "changeup in the signal."

In training, the variables are exercise selection, intensity, volume, and rest intervals. These are undulated throughout the off-season, preseason, and in season, and, if lucky enough, through the postseason.

An Outline of the Broncos' First Workout

Part I: The Warm-Up

We began with a full active dynamic warm-up that consisted of isolated and integrated movements for total body preparation. These skills are used to reinforce coordination and common motor skills that are used for sporting action such as acceleration, deceleration, and change of direction.

Isolated movements, or activation exercises, are segmental movements that allow for low-level contraction to "wake up the muscles" or to enhance the mind-body connection. This will, in turn, allow for faster contractions while providing a tool for realignment of the body to allow for more efficiency. This leads to a healthier and faster athlete.

Integration exercises are meant to move the body in a more dynamic multi-planed fashion to prepare the athlete for the ballistic and variable demands of sport.

From various squat and lunge patterns, I have the athletes go through multiple skips and sprint mimicking drills that ultimately prepare the body for the training session.

Squats (beginner). Feet between hip width and shoulder width. Feet straight ahead or toes slightly out (symmetrical). Initiate range of motion with hips back as the knees flex and lower the center of mass. Shoulders and shins should advance slightly forward. Hold slight pause at end of range of motion. Push through the feet into the ground to ascend back to the fully extended position. Repeat for number of reps for goal of the workout without compromising technique.

Squats weighted (intermediate) using barbell, dumbbell, sandbell. Feet between hip width and shoulder width. Feet straight ahead or toes slightly out (symmetrical). Initiate range of motion with hips back as the knees flex and lower the center of mass. Shoulders and shins should advance slightly forward. Hold slight pause at the end of range of motion. Push through the feet into the ground to ascend back to the fully extended position. Repeat for the number of reps for goal of the workout without compromising technique.

Squat with asymmetrical load (intermediate, advanced) dumbbell, sandbell. Feet between hip width and shoulder width. Feet straight ahead or toes slightly out (symmetrical). Initiate range of motion with hips back as the knees flex and lower the center of mass. Shoulders and shins should advance slightly forward. Hold slight pause at the end of range of motion. Push through the feet into the ground to ascend back to the fully extended position. Repeat for the number of reps for goal of the workout without compromising technique.

Squat jumps (advanced) with sandbell/dumbbell. Feet hip width. Feet straight ahead or toes slightly out (symmetrical). Quickly drop into a squat position. Rapidly reverse the squat and push through the feet into the ground explosively. Try to achieve as much vertical height as possible with the alignment of ear through ankle at apex. Land in quarter-squat position with feet flat and core braced.

Part II: Motor Skills Training

As the workout continued we progressed the drill to include transitional movements from a multi-planar drill to linear acceleration. Sports are played in spots of acceleration. The goal is to master acceleration from various starting positions. I believe in doing all of the right things from the wrong positions, meaning, in sports we are never going to be in the exact spot, but if we have mastered our footwork and our ability to accelerate, we have the tools to get into the right position. This phase consisted of general footwork drills conducted with agility ladders.

Eric Decker does the footwork tapioca prior to an explosive acceleration.

Dawkins bursting into acceleration after tapioca footwork.

Our work-to-rest ratios were 1:5, meaning if we did 6 seconds of work, I would allow 30 seconds of rest on average.

Part III: The Cooldown

At the conclusion of the workout, we finished with a barefoot cooldown. I believe our cooldown increases the body's ability to recover for the next session. Barefoot allows the athlete to increase the integrity of the foot, which can alleviate many chronic ankle, knee, and hip injuries athletes develop from sports.

Camp Dawkins

There were no coaches around to impress. The lockout had halted that notion.

No local television cameras were there to keep them honest. The media had not been invited.

Yet, the fifteen Broncos who showed up for the first player-supervised team workout on May 10 at the South Suburban Sports Dome—otherwise known as the bubble—attacked each conditioning drill as if they were trying to make the team.

The Broncos, who were so bad the season before that they wound up with the number two overall draft pick, were on their way to building an AFC West team while nobody was watching.

"Hey, why come out here if you're not going to go 100 percent?" said Joe Mays, who would use these lockout workouts, and three previous years of NFL experience, to hold off third-round drafted rookie Nate Irving and become the Broncos' starting middle linebacker. "We're all out here competing. Competing amongst ourselves to be the best player we can. Competing against each other."

Loren Landow loved that. People might have the wrong idea about performance coaches. Their job doesn't begin and end with training, fitness, strengthening, and conditioning.

When the Broncos' director of strength and conditioning position became available prior to the 2012 season, Landow was one of just two men who were granted an interview with the Broncos football hierarchy trio of John Elway, John Fox, and Brian Xanders.

Elway, Fox, and Xanders wanted to know: Why, Mr. Landow, would you be interested in this job? With Steadman Hawkins, Landow was essentially his own boss. He worked privately and in groups with more than 250 athletes.

The agents would pay Steadman Hawkins for their services, and then Landow would get a percentage. He had flexibility in his work schedule. He could work out Tim Tebow twice a week, then head to London to finish off the training with Olympic swimmer Missy Franklin, another of his clients, in July.

He would lose all of that if he became the Broncos' strength-and-conditioning director. The team would ask him to work from 5:30 a.m. to 9 p.m. during training camp. He would have to work every day for seven consecutive months, take a month off, and then come back and work long hours, seven days a week, for three more months.

Elway, Fox, and Xanders wanted to know: Why?

"Because I want to win," Landow said.

That is Loren Landow. A man, but more than that. One of those men who always competes. Whether it was fighting to get well enough to never see a hospital bed again as a child, whether it was baseball or wrestling, whether it was oral quizzes at the family dinner table, whether it was competing in drug-free bodybuilding competitions, Landow wanted to play ball.

And he wanted to win.

The Broncos triumvirate were left impressed by Landow but chose the other candidate, Luke Richesson, who had a few more NFL connections after working the previous three years as strength-and-conditioning director of the Jacksonville Jaguars.

But in the previous summer of 2011, with no other Broncos coaches around, Landow was the only coach the Broncos players had.

Said Landow: "I was excited. But I also had one of those feelings of, 'OK, did I just bite off more than I can chew?' And then the concern was, 'What am I getting them ready for? I'm just going to have them run around and break a little sweat for one week, two weeks? Or is it going to be something bigger than that, which is training for the entire off-season?'"

There's a lesson there. It's OK to fear the unknown. It's natural to experience apprehension about change or venturing into something new. But fear and apprehension are feelings. Not stop signs.

This would be the first time Landow had directed a group on this scale. He'd always had large off-season NFL training groups of twenty to thirty guys. He'd run camps for high school-aged athletes. And he'd been running NFL combine prep training for almost fifteen years.

So it wasn't the size of the group that tested Landow's nerves. It was the circumstances of the group. They had no income, no health insurance, no consistent training after the season, which left them in multiple states of physical fitness. NFLPA executive director DeMaurice Smith even told the players that their health insurance was going to be canceled by the league, and that it was important to protect themselves and their families.

Said Landow: "The first workout, I knew I had to leave an impression on the guys. I wanted to instill the importance of my warm-up. My warm-up is probably my most valuable tool that I have as a practitioner. Just because of what it can do on injury prevention and the postural restoration side of things."

Quadruped series (fire hydrants). On all fours with hands under shoulders and knees under hips. Core braced and arms straight, lift work leg to side 20–30 degrees. Hold at end range for 2 seconds and return to start position. 6–8 repetitions.

Quadruped series (hip circles). On all fours with hands under the shoulders and knees under hips. Core braced and arms straight, in either clockwise or counterclockwise, circle the knee about the hip joint. 6–8 repetitions.

Quadruped series (scorpion). On all fours with hands under the shoulders and knees under the hips. Core braced and arms straight maintaining a knee joint angle at 90 degrees, lift the work leg into extension. Hold at end range for 2 seconds and return to start position. 6–8 repetitions.

Quadruped series (lateral leg reach). On all fours with hands under the shoulders and knees under the hips. Extend one leg fully while laterally flexing leg slightly, externally rotate so toe is pointing neutral. Maintain a braced core with arms straight. Hold at end range for 2 seconds and return to start position. 6–8 repetitions.

Straight-leg series (supine high kick). On back with one leg straight and one
bent. Core braced, squeeze the quadriceps of the straight leg and lift with the
hip flexor as high as possible without altering pelvic or knee position. Hold at
end range for 2 seconds and return to start position. 6–8 repetitions.

Straight-leg series (side-lying abduction). On side with alignment from ear to ankle, with foot dorsi-flexed and slight internal rotation of thigh. Core braced, squeeze the quadriceps of the work leg and lift to 30 degrees of abduction while maintaining alignment. Hold at end range for 2 seconds and return to start position. 6–8 repetitions.

Straight-leg series (side-lying adduction). On side with alignment from ear to ankle. Figure four the top leg to expose the bottom leg. Lift the down leg 2–4" off the ground. Hold at end range for 2 seconds and return to start position. 6–8 repetitions.

Straight-leg series (prone abduction). On stomach with forehead resting on hand. Lift work leg 2" in extension with the glutes. With foot dorsi-flexed, abduct the leg 20 degrees. Hold at end range for 2 seconds and return to start position. 6–8 repetitions.

Postural restoration? "Basically, it means within playing a sport you run into deficient patterns of posture. Dysfunction of posture will eventually lead to injury. What I'm trying to do is essentially restore their alignment, if you will."

Whether the city of Rome or an athlete's biomotor skills, neither can be built in a day. Here's what Landow saw in some of the Broncos players who attended the team workouts:

J. D. Walton, starting center: "Every offensive lineman has to work on better knee bend (good ankle ranges of motion typically lead to better knee bend), which is when they have that better leverage. The key is to understand biomechanics."

For this, Landow consulted with offensive line coaches. He's had numerous conversations over the years with Alex Gibbs, the Broncos' longtime offensive line coach, and Jerry Wampfler, the longtime offensive line coach with several NFL teams.

Gibbs was Landow's type of line coach. Gibbs loved the smaller, more athletic offensive lineman. Blockers who were nimble in their movements. Landow made a living on improving nimble mobility.

Zane Beadles, starting left guard: "Big kid, wanted to work on his knee bend. Footwork, upper body strength, and core strength."

With almost all offensive linemen, improving knee bend is a key component to their training. How do you improve knee bend? Number 1: Increase ankle mobility. The ankle allows the shin to move forward further, which allows the femur to sit back lower. It is like a seesaw. The shin moves forward, the femur moves back. This allowed the blocker to get his butt lower and create great knee bend.

Chris Clark, offensive tackle who often played tight end in the Broncos' "power" running formations during the season: "I know I'm starting to sound like a broken record, but knee bend. The taller guys are harder to bend at knees, bend at the waist. When they don't have that bend, they get off-balanced. They just don't have a strong base."

Chris Kuper, starting right guard: "I've worked with Kupe for two or three years now. He's got great knee bend, great footwork. I just wanted to increase his fitness levels."

Matt Willis, Broncos No. 4 receiver and special teams standout: "He's got straight-line speed and reaction. I worked with him on change of direction at full speed."

Joe Mays, starting middle linebacker: "We wanted him learning how to accelerate from all positions. Close the gap, close the distance. Joe is big and strong, but we wanted him to be more efficient to the ball. He's pretty good going forward."

Cassius Vaughn, starting left cornerback when Champ Bailey shifted to nickel through the first five games of the year: "Speed. Cassius is a freak. Great speed, great footwork. Sometimes he gets his feet out of position on change of direction. He's always straight-line fast."

Spencer Larsen, starting fullback: "Good athlete. Good balance. Wanted to work on his reaction, quick burst speed, acceleration speed."

Eric Decker, starting receiver: "Talk about a guy who has great body position. Great body control. We wanted to work on him becoming more efficient off the line. He runs such deliberate routes. He shocked me how fast he was."

Eddie Royal, starting receiver: "He was hurt when he joined our group. He was coming off hip surgery, so we were teaching him proper warm-ups and acceleration mechanics to help minimize the strain on his hip."

Julius Thomas, rookie tight end: "Freakishly good athlete. Long. Great short speed, soft hands, great body positioning."

(There were concerns that after playing four years of basketball at Portland State, and just one season of football, Thomas would not be much of a blocker and handle the physical grind of the NFL. But after Landow set eyes on Thomas for a few days, the performance coach semi-joked that he would not bother having Thomas block. He'd just send him down the hash marks, have the quarterback throw up the ball, and let Thomas's athleticism take it from there.)

Brady Quinn, backup quarterback: "Can't say enough good things about him. A leader, first and foremost. Athletic, big and strong, always in great shape. We were just trying to maximize his performance in all areas."

Kyle Orton, starting quarterback: "Kyle would come in and do his work. Never complain. He would come in to Steadman Hawkins with Kuper a couple times. He was always very polite. He is what he is on the speed side. He's got good precise footwork. Not necessarily the fastest, but very precise."

Lance Ball, No. 3 running back who would move to No. 2 after Knowshon Moreno blew out his knee early in game 9 at Kansas City. Ball would get thirty carries in that 17–10 win at K.C.: "Explosive. Those first 5 to 10 yards he's very explosive. One of the more explosive I've seen within 5 yards. There's quick, there's fast, there's explosive. He might miss the hole once in a while. But he has a lot of power, a low center of mass."

Brian Dawkins, starting strong safety: "He was a leader. When he came in the room, a lot of young guys turned and listened. He has very fast feet. I was shocked. The biggest thing to work on was closing speed in transition to acceleration. Footwork, lateral movement."

Robert Ayers, starting defensive end: "He came in at the end with a knee injury: Big body, pretty good feet. Had glimpses of great athleticism."

Short steps, high knees, quick steps, quick, quick, quick. And then, with a little prodding from Landow, the players would complete their footwork drill through the ropes by exploding into a sprint.

No one loafed through the first organized workout of Broncos players. No one pulled a too-cool-for-school, who-needs-this attitude. Every player brought full effort on every drill. Should have heard the huffing, seen the sweat dripping.

No wonder these guys made it to the NFL.

"Soon enough, we will all be in position where we will be trying to make the team, whether at minicamp or training camp or whatever," Dawkins said. "So why not go all out now?"

Quarterback Kyle Orton showed up early to throw to receiver Eric Decker. Other projected starters who attended were center J. D. Walton, left guard Zane Beadles, defensive tackle Kevin Vickerson, middle linebacker Joe Mays, and defensive end Robert Ayers. Cornerback Cassius Vaughn and offensive tackle Chris Clark—two players who were on the Broncos' roster through the 2011 season—were also there.

Not present were Tim Tebow and Brady Quinn, established workout warriors and Orton's competition at quarterback. Tebow was working out on his own and with quarterback coaching guru Zeke Bratkowski. Quinn was also working out on his own and with quarterback coach David Lee.

Tebow's absence, though, drew criticism from local radio talk-show hosts. Why? Because Tebow doesn't walk down a street without generating mentions from fifteen Twitter feeds. Because Orton was there. And because Tebow was also seen starring in numerous TV commercials and hawking his autobiography on a book tour.

The commercials and book tour didn't look good. Not when the team was working out and he wasn't. That was the perception, anyway. It was not reality.

The guff Tebow took for not attending the first team-organized workout irked Dawkins.

"I know you guys took attendance and all that, but this was not a get-here-at-all-costs type of thing," Dawkins said. "This is not about one way being the right way, or another way is the wrong way. This is about providing a safe haven for those who want to come out and work."

Von Miller, who the Broncos selected the previous week with the number 2 overall draft pick, and the rest of the new batch of Broncos rookies were also absent. The only rookie who showed initiative in seeking out how to attend the Dawkins camp was Julius Thomas, a fourth-round tight end. Thomas would show up at the organized players' camp in mid-June.

While the Broncos who attended that first team-workout session tried hard, Landow warned against trying too hard. As one of the nation's top performance coaches, Landow is constantly instructing his athletes to stop trying so hard and start focusing on technique.

Said Landow: "In that first workout, I was doing a lot of footwork, and then I would transition it into acceleration. One of my biggest philosophies in any sport that's ground-based is we don't go into acceleration and the play is over. You need some sort of a footwork component, like in a lateral or multidirectional plane, and then we have to find out how to transition from that multidirectional pattern into acceleration."

And for all the impressive effort the Broncos players were putting into Landow's workout, inefficient movement patterns became evident.

Landow: "Everybody was so inefficient at it. Everybody was. I sat there and thought: This is my opportunity to show these guys how and why I can help. Early on in the process you don't want to lose guys like Brian by beating your chest and saying: 'You need me.' But I can clearly show these guys that being who I am—who is not the athlete they are—how much more efficient and quicker I was because I was always in the right positions."

There is working out during the off-season. And as some players found out, there is the Landow workout.

"That was tough," said Mays, his shirt drenched with sweat.

"I've been working out with Dawk this whole off-season, but that was a good test there."

Landow is big on motion and agility. Some of Landow's new clients are more agile than others, but all gave the same amount of effort.

With the NFL essentially shut down during the 2011 off-season, with the exception of a three-day rookie draft, a few teams started player-supervised workouts in late April.

Dawkins started making preliminary plans for the player-supervised workout in April but wanted to wait until the 8th Circuit Court of Appeals in St. Louis ruled on whether to "stay" a previous ruling by Minnesota Judge Susan Nelson that the owner-imposed lockout should be lifted.

With no such ruling made, Dawkins decided, stay or no stay, let's go. On May 10, Camp Dawkins was on. Loren Landow was the director.

"All of us are training, all of us are working, so in a sense if we do come together, nothing would change as far as what we're doing now," Dawkins said. "But we would be able to build camaraderie by working out together."

After his first 45-minute workout with the Broncos players, Landow was pleased with the effort but not satisfied with the results. There were a couple of things about this group he didn't like. One, he quickly detected a potential focus problem during the warm-up. And two, there was a clear deficiency in technique during most of the explosion drills.

But Landow didn't speak up. Not that he can't. Not that he hasn't. He's not a barker, anyway. But those coaches who bark a lot: after a while, it always sounds like noise. Noise that can be tuned out.

Landow is an instructor, a teacher.

Landow: "I let that happen for a couple weeks. I didn't say anything. I wanted them to see I was consistent, that I was always there early, always prepared, and had a reason for what they were doing. I wanted them to get to know me a little bit. If I said something early on, I would have lost them."

About the third week into the Camp Dawkins workouts, though, Landow let the players know a little more sternly who they were and why they needed to be there.

CHAPTER 5

Media Day

CAMERAS POINTED silently but purposely at the large young men clad in shorts, T-shirts, and top-of-the-line sneakers.

Cameras on tripods, cameras on shoulders, notebook toters, TV reporters, sports radio talk-show hosts, bloggers. The media "personalities" were dressed in a wide range of fashion, from high-heeled boots and fur coats (one) to jeans and tennis shoes (everybody else).

Media members blanketed the near wall, almost from end to end, at the South Suburban Sports Dome.

Starved for anything related to the NFL and Broncos during the league's labor lockout—even if it was nothing more than grown men skipping, running through ladders, conditioning, sweating, drills and more drills that did not include the football itself—Denver's media descended upon Camp Dawkins.

Word was out. The first Broncos players-only workout was held May 10, 2011. Training camp, if it was to go off on time, would be six weeks away. At the invitation of both Judianne Atencio and Loren Landow, *Denver Post* beat reporter Mike Klis was allowed to observe the first team-organized, no-coach workout.

Klis wrote it up, sent it on, and the paper published it the next morning.

Wednesday, May 11, was an off day for the Broncos players—Landow believes in recovery—but not for Atencio, who fielded one call after another from hungry Denver media outlets.

At Atencio's respectful urging, and against Landow's concern, Camp Dawkins would host a Media Day on Thursday, May 13.

Landow is built along the lines of a small, skill-position player, but he has the mentality of an offensive lineman. Sweat and guts. Forget the glory. Skill-position players, particularly at receiver and running back, crave the spotlight. Most offensive linemen pride themselves on performing duty without attention.

Said Landow of inviting the media to his workout sessions: "I was apprehensive. I was pretty reluctant. I was intent on sending the players a message on why they needed this. I didn't want Media Day to distract from the fact that we were just getting to know each other from trainer to athlete, and I didn't want it to be a circus. I thought we had a great first workout (on Tuesday, May 11), and I didn't want it to hurt my chances of further bonding with these guys."

After all, the subtitle of this book is *Building a Championship Team (While Nobody's Watching)*. The media would now be looking. And the media's purpose was to bring the workouts to the public. Media Day meant everyone would be watching, at least as presented in snippets on the ten o'clock news.

But whether it's holiday shopping season when the credit cards have been pushed to the max since Memorial Day, or you are supposed to be bedridden with a contagious virus on an unseasonably beautiful day, life is often about choosing between contradictions.

Landow had hired Atencio, after all. As head of one of the most efficient small PR firms in the country, Judianne's numerous high-profile athletes included former Broncos quarterbacks Jake Plummer and Jay Cutler.

Atencio is not hired to stay quiet. She is hired to spread the word. For Loren Landow, his desire for intensity and focus was understandable. But a business that relies on word of mouth can only grow so much.

And it's not like Atencio wanted Media Day to make a star of Landow. If name recognition was a side benefit, so be it. But her heart and purpose were in the right place. She sincerely wanted Broncos fans, of which there are millions, to realize their players were not sloughing off.

Said Landow: "Judianne really convinced me it was a necessary evil where I'm more focused at the task at hand. I'm, 'Let's not have anything distract what we're doing.' Then she said, 'Hey, why don't we let fans know—why don't we let the organization know—we're taking this seriously?'"

Through no fault of his own, whenever Tim Tebow is part of a team, the story is no longer about the team. It's about Tebow. The term "superstar" is thrown around a tad loosely in sports.

Almost never is an athlete a true star outside of his own sport. A featured NBA game of the week will draw a tiny audience. How, then, can LeBron James and Kobe Bryant be considered superstars?

Mick Jagger is a superstar. Jack Nicholson is a superstar.

Tim Tebow? Truly a superstar. Thousands of moms, grandmas, accountants, non-sports enthusiasts found themselves on fall Sundays wondering, "How'd Tebow do?"

So when Camp Dawkins opened on May 10, and the *Denver Post* took roll call on the participants, the media antennas (sports talk hosts and TV sports anchors) did not spend much time talking about who was there—but who wasn't.

The primary topic around the Denver-area coffee machines in mid-May: Where's Tebow? Why isn't Tebow working out with his teammates? Shouldn't Tebow be out there working on his passing mechanics?

Tebow was working out, of course, and probably more diligently than anyone else.

But Tebow had a bit of a perception problem. The lockout coincided with the release of his autobiography, *Through My Eyes*, a rare sports book that transcended the typical football audience and crossed over to book-buying popularity. Read: Women.

Want to write a book that sells? Rule number one is to write a book that appeals to the female audience, especially in fiction. According to a National Public Radio (NPR) study in 2007, women account for roughly 80 percent of the fiction market. Men do represent the majority of biography readers, though. Tebow's book was a biography that appealed to both sexes. *Through My Eyes* instantly went to the national best-seller lists, selling roughly 185,000 copies in its first eight months.

The book tour, coupled with Tebow's Jockey television commercials, created the impression he was too busy to work out with his teammates.

None of Tebow's teammates were bothered by his absence. But they were aware of what stirred the town's buzz.

"Tell Tim Tebow we're looking for him," Broncos running back LenDale White said playfully after the Media Day workout on May 13.

Further hurting Tebow was that while his absence was duly noted, Kyle Orton was present and accounted for. Orton had what Tebow's legion of followers wanted Tebow to have: the Broncos' starting quarterback position.

About 45 minutes before the team's player-supervised workout began Thursday at the South Suburban Sports Dome, Orton arrived to throw passes to wide receiver Eric Decker and tight end Dan Gronkowski.

"He throws a great catchable ball," said Gronkowski, meaning a pass that has zip but is soft on the hands.

"He understands, too, that you have to make your throw go over the linemen, so he was really working on his release point in game situations," Decker said.

Orton threw at the far end of the dome, as far from the attending media contingent as possible. He then left, without comment, before the rest of the Dawkins-organized team workout with Landow began.

The *Denver Post* again took roll for the Media Day session, labeling the group as Brian's Bunch: Running backs Lance Ball and LenDale White; offensive linemen Zane Beadles, J. D. Walton, Jeff Byers, and Chris Clark; defensive backs Brian Dawkins and Cassius Vaughn; defensive linemen Kevin Vickerson and Ben Garland (who was serving his military commitment with the Air Force); linebacker Joe Mays; Decker, Gronkowski, and Orton.

Not a Saints-like turnout, but, then, Dawkins let his teammates know they had no obligation to attend the workouts, especially if they were out of town. During the NFL lockout, the Broncos weren't paying to fly in players and house them, as they would for organized team activities or minicamps during a normal off-season. Many of the players, especially the new batch of rookies, don't have housing set up and can't afford to stay long term at a hotel.

Dawkins tried to tell the media the workouts were NOT mandatory.

That did not stop the starved beast that was the Denver media. Tebow felt pressured and would show up a week later. He had been working out plenty on his own, and with various quarterback coaches who gave him personal instruction in trying to fix his throwing mechanics. But the guff from the Denver media can be a powerful thing. He admitted he was pushed into attending Camp Dawkins not by Dawkins, not by Landow, not by any of his teammates, but by the criticism he was receiving from the Denver media and fan base.

Whatever it takes.

Once Brian Dawkins commits, he not only participates: he buys lunch.

Dawkins picked up the Sports Dome rent bill, Landow's trainer fees, and the lunch that Atencio provided for every player who participated in the Broncos-only workouts.

Former Broncos star Rod Smith was impressed.

"What he's doing here is very smart, very professional," Smith said. "I can promise you, you can never work yourself out the way somebody else will."

Smith, who hosts his own podcast sports show, attended the Media Day workout session. Smith had retired following the 2007 season as the Broncos' all-time leader in receptions, receiving yards, and receiving touchdowns.

Smith will be formally inducted into the Broncos' Ring of Fame at halftime in week 3 of the 2012 season. Like all former players, though, Smith aligns himself with the "player" fraternity rather than the "media" fraternity.

The biggest reason why active players stiff-arm the media is because, for the most part, every member of the media is charged with "telling it like it is." The truth can hurt, especially when delivered in the form of critiqued performance.

Still, Dawkins didn't have much reservation about Media Day. To Landow, who was accustomed to training his clients well away from the public's gaze, the media were strangers. To Dawkins, who had been performing in the spotlight for almost his entire life, the media were at least a familiar acquaintance, if not necessarily a friend or foe.

The media had thickened Dawkins's skin, numbed some of his feelings.

"This is going to sound crazy, but I wanted to keep things as routine as we could," Dawkins said about the Media Day session. "When you first come in to work out with the team during the off-season, usually there's media there and people want to talk to guys. So that was not anything different from what we normally experience at a voluntary conditioning camp.

"I wanted guys to be able to get their two cents in with the media, but after that it's work. We were there to prepare for a season. We were preparing to win the (AFC) West."

Landow understood, but his biggest reservation was the timing.

Said Landow: "My thought was, 'Let's allow the guys to get their legs under them.' Some guys needed to get some fitness under their belt before the media was watching and be able to pick them apart if they were out of shape."

For the most part, the players attacked Landow's drills with fervor. There was no coasting. One player went at it hard. The next player went at it hard.

The players' intensity impressed the media, who mostly delivered positive reviews. By extension, the media were impressed with Landow.

Said Landow, "I remember (Fox 31 sports director) Chris Tanaka, he asked, 'Can we have a couple questions with you?' I said, 'Sure.' And the second he asked that, I had twelve cameras in my face. Probably thirty reporters gathered around asking questions like: 'What do we hope to get out of this?' 'What's your objective?' And then a lot of questions on the conditioning of the team in the past and why they may have had mid- to late-season drop-offs. I pretty much left those questions as, 'No comment.' But they were definitely probing."

Why the Broncos had a habit of fading in the final month of the season became subject for debate and theory. What was indisputable was that so many promising Broncos seasons wilted into disappointment.

- In 2011, the Broncos were 8–5. They finished 8–8.
- They were 6–0 in 2009 and then 8–4. The Broncos lost eight of their last ten, including the final four in a row.
- They were 3–0 in 2008 and then 8–5 with a three-game lead and three games to go. They finished 8–8 and out of the play-offs.
- The Broncos were 2–0 in 2007 and then 5–5. They went out 2–4.

- They were 7–2 in 2006, only to go 2–5 down the stretch.
- In 2004, the Broncos started 5–1. They wound up 10–6 and got creamed by Indianapolis (and future Broncos quarterback Peyton Manning) in the first round of the play-offs.
- In 2003, they started 4–0. They wound up 10–6 and got smoked again by Indianapolis (and Manning) in the first round of the play-offs.
- In 2002, the Broncos started 3–0 and 6–2. They went 3–5 in the second half and missed the play-offs.
- In 2001, they started 2–0 and finished 8–8.

In short, the Broncos started strong and staggered to the finish in nine of their past eleven seasons. Even in their Super Bowl seasons, the Broncos were 11–2 in 1997 and finished 1–2, and 13–0 in 1998 before losing two of their final three.

Could Landow's training techniques address these final-month swoons? Landow knew that the earlier and more consistent the team could start training in the off-season, the longer they would be able to retain their fitness and athleticism throughout the season. At the moment, he had other concerns. A couple of media types were a little too friendly with the players. Although the players meant business, the media detected a looser atmosphere at Camp Dawkins than the closely guarded practice sessions at Dove Valley.

Like a kid with a hall pass and no hall monitor in sight, the Denver media had a little more fun in communicating with the players.

Landow wanted full attention for an hour, but still he felt good about his first two sessions with Camp Dawkins. He had the players' attention. And the players were responding to his instruction.

And then Landow watched the ten o'clock news. Uh-oh.

I had watched a little bit of the footage on the news on how it was interpreted of what we were doing. I think that was the biggest reason why I said no more media. Because they weren't interpreting guys in the best light of what they were doing. We were there working out a full hour, hour and a half, and the segments that were being shown were guys jacking around after the session. That was exactly the message we did not want to send to the fans and the organization. If you're there for the workout, capture the workout. Don't show guys kicking soccer balls before or after the workout or wrestling each other. I thought it was a slap in the face to the players and what we were trying to accomplish.

Working out in front of the media's glare was halted as soon as it began. Dawkins had texted Atencio prior to Media Day: Do it once, let the fans know we are working, and be done. The media would occasionally descend upon the parking lot at South Suburban Sports Dome and catch a player going in or out of their workout for a sound bite or interview.

But the Camp Dawkins workouts themselves would go back behind closed doors.

The Broncos would spend their lockout seeking to win the AFC West title while no one was watching.

CHAPTER 6

The Grind

AMONG CURRENT BRONCOS, their longest-serving offensive player is also Loren Landow's longest-tenured client.

Right guard Chris Kuper decided to skip the final semester of his senior year at North Dakota in 2006 so he could concentrate on bettering his chances for a job in the NFL.

These days, most draftable prospects make this same, life-impacting decision. They are so close to earning a college diploma. But more than people realize, getting that degree is often in conflict with a once-in-a-lifetime opportunity to play their sport at the highest, or professional, level.

Ultimately, the student-athlete must address that enormous fork by asking: Why do you get a college degree in the first place?

Almost always, the answer is to get the best, highest-paying job possible. Name an occupation in the real world that is more enjoyable, or is better paying, than professional football player?

Kuper, through his Colorado Springs–based agents Craig Domann and Leo Goeas, packed up what few belongings he had in Grand Forks and temporarily transplanted to Denver where he

Chris Kuper, Jeff Byers, Russ Hochstein in game stance prepare to pull to the left.

would work out with highly recommended pre-combine trainer Loren Landow.

Kuper didn't know Denver. He didn't know Landow. He didn't know what he was getting himself into. He was twenty-three years old.

What would you do?

"I just thought if I was going to play football, I would go for it," Kuper said. "It was night and day from my college strength coach. For me, everything was about volume in college. The more reps you did, the more sit-ups you did: that's how we were measured. Loren, he individualizes it to how your body feels, how you have to perform in certain scenarios. Once you get to the end of it, everybody's got to be in this box, which is the combine. So you train for that."

Kuper, whose quickness and agility for his size made him an ideal fit for the zone-blocking scheme run by then-coach Mike Shanahan, was the Broncos' fifth-round draft pick in 2006. He became a starter in 2007, signed a six-year, $28 million contract extension in 2010, and was instrumental in galvanizing the Broncos' lockout workouts of 2011.

See, while it took the strong persona of Dawkins to organize the Broncos-only lockout workouts, it was Kuper who led all Broncos to Landow. Once the lockout was officially on in mid-March, Kuper called his offensive line mates together for workouts, first at the Big Bear Ice Arena, then at Sports Xcel, and finally at what all Broncos know as the bubble.

"More so it was, 'If you guys are in town, I know this great trainer,'" Kuper said. "I've been with him for a long time. It's nice to have guys with like body type, who play the same positions and you can compete with on some of the drills."

That was the amazing thing about these Landow-led workouts. Even though the stern eyes of Broncos coaches were not upon them, these players went at Landow's drills hard. There was no jacking around, at least not in the drills portion.

"In a team sport what motivates you is competing with your teammates. That's why during the lockout, if you were to lift and run solely by yourself, I don't think you would have pushed yourself mentally quite as hard as when you see another guy next to you going at it," Kuper said.

Offensive linemen and defensive linemen, with the high school players in the background, do footwork drills at Valor Christian High School.

Eventually, the Broncos' off-season workouts returned to normal. As normal as they could be during an abnormal off-season of the NFL lockout.

There would be another media spike when star quarterback Tim Tebow showed up for his first Landow-directed training session on May 19.

But for the most part, Camp Dawkins became about sweat and strength, agility and quickness, conditioning, and bonding. Stuff that doesn't make for good television, even if it does lead to a better football player.

The lockout was dragging on. It began in mid-March, was forgotten somewhat by the anticipation of the late-April draft and the influx of new talent—highly touted rookies coming in to take away jobs from established veterans—and the lockout remained inert through mid-May.

The lockout was now two months old, and a resolution seemed to be at least two more months away. If the owners and union officials did not seem to have a sense of urgency about reaching a labor accord in May, why would June be any different? Or early July?

These labor disputes always seemed to operate on a calendar, and the calendar always seemed to have crossed-out boxes upon x-ed out boxes.

Why is it during any labor dispute, negotiations never really get serious until the eleventh hour of the thirtieth day?

NFL players were officially in their dead zone. The cameras were gone. The occasional reporter such as Channel 9's Susie Wargin would wait in the parking lot to interview a player for an off-season profile piece.

But the workouts themselves had become a sequestered exercise. The energy created by the initial Broncos-only workouts had dissipated, leaving the players to rely on little else but self-motivation.

This is when Landow decided to lace a tad more gravity into his coach-side manner.

"You guys warm up like a 4–12 team," Landow said one day.

Joe Mays, Cassius Vaughn, and Matt Willis were among the few who were watching and listening to Landow. So Landow directed his comments at them. Mays, Vaughn, and Willis caught it: Loren was noticeably irritated.

Said Landow: "Everybody was talking. Nobody was listening or following instructions; how you prepare is how you perform, focused effort! The habit of listening is key to being coachable. I had showed these guys through the first couple weeks that I was consistent. I was always on time. I always had everything set up. I always had the workout planned out.

"Now, I was asking them to be consistent. College guys understand it. They get it. They get it because they have to get it."

Landow, remember, wasn't interested in merely getting his hometown Broncos players to a higher fitness level, or bigger muscles. If that's all he was in it for, he'd train the spouses and children of Denver's wealthy.

Joe Mays and Cassius Vaughn prepare the body with dynamic flexibility "elbow to instep" prior to a hard conditioning session.

Landow wants to win. He wants the Broncos to win. And the last time Landow watched the Broncos play, they had just finished a 4–12 season.

Call a player old. Call a player inexperienced. Call a player tiny or heavy or slow. Just don't call him a player on a 4–12 team. That's like calling a player a loser. Never call a player a loser.

Landow's comment—you warm up like a 4–12 team—hit 'em where it hurt.

"It did get under our skins a little bit," Mays said. "It woke a lot of guys up. We had that mentality where we were going through the motions. That's pretty much what happened that (2010) season. We went through the motions. We didn't really go out and do anything to make us better.

"The way we played the season before—it was one of those things we needed to hear."

Ordinarily, Landow keeps it loose. He can cut up with the best of them. He creates an atmosphere where players *want* to work, *want* to work out. Look forward to working out.

There isn't a person in America, especially around the New Year, who hasn't gotten fired up to work out. But are they fired up in week two? Do they still look forward to dragging themselves to the gym by mid-February?

Eventually, working out stirs feelings closer to drudgery than excitement. Where Landow is able to keep his players interested is in the results.

Mays noticed how Landow's running techniques improved his explosion. Cassius Vaughn could tell he was quicker to the ball merely because of his improved foot transfer.

Landow kept it loose, sure. But pay attention when he's all business and you'll learn something.

Said Landow: "I could show the guys that by accelerating with the wrong foot when they were coming out of a break was making them slower—and that's huge when you look at a defensive guy.

Loren being interviewed by the media. Well over thirty members of the Denver media showed up at the second workout. The goal was to show the fans and the Broncos' organization that the players weren't taking the lockout as an extended vacation, but as a time to get better and prepare for the upcoming season. Copyright © Eric Lars Bakke.

Brian Dawkins addresses members of the media on Media Day. Brian's main objective was to remind the media that the workouts were not mandatory, but that it was an opportunity for guys to get together, train together, and build a camaraderie while the lockout was in effect. Copyright © Eric Lars Bakke.

Denver Broncos' Justin Bannin works on his reaction, agility, and acceleration with reactive light sensors. This encourages one-on-one competition that challenges the athletes to be quicker than the opposition.

Running the steps at Red Rocks, Denver Broncos' Joel Dreessen is really emphasizing good acceleration mechanics to maximize hip and leg power.

Chris Kuper and Buffalo Bills' Eric Pears work on first-step acceleration with resisted A runs. One of Loren's consistent coaching points all summer was to be the master of acceleration in ten yards, as most plays are either won or lost within that distance. The more efficient each player is in that distance, the greater chance of winning the one-on-one battles against your opposition.

Denver Broncos' Eric Decker, Luke Snapp, and Loren Landow discuss the next drill for the workout. Landow is a big believer in explaining the hows and the whys to his athletes for better buy-in.

Brady Quinn on the home stretch of the conditioning test. Assuming the players would be put through the conditioning test of years past, once a week they would prepare for it—not making it the training focus, but making sure all could pass with flying colors. This particular test was 300-yard shuttle with finishing times between .45 and .62 depending on position. Rest was three minutes; then, the test was repeated three times.

Brady Quinn runs the two-minute drill after the workout; two to three times per week Brady would run the guys through the high-paced tempo of the two-minute. Chris Clark, Chris Kuper, J. D. Walton, Zane Beadles, and Eric Decker run the drill while Loren Landow and Brian Dawkins watch from the sidelines.

Loren talks with Brian Dawkins prior to the session as the players do a dynamic flexibility exercise called "Rockers," a great active stretch for the low back and hamstrings.

Joe Mays leads the group (Eric Decker, Cassius Vaughn, Rob Gronkowski, Lance Ball, Brian Dawkins, and Ben Garland) in a dynamic flexibility exercise, lateral A skip. The intent is to rehearse a rhythmic pattern with opposing limbs while simulating the toe-up, knee-up, and heel-up mechanics in acceleration.

Chris Kuper, Jeff Byers, and Russ Hochstein pull on Loren's cue. Quick first step and good acceleration mechanics can probably benefit the offensive lineman as much as any position on the field. The game is won in the "trenches"; and if the offensive lineman can reach the second level faster, he can chip away at the one-on-one battles against the defense.

Players catch their breath while Brady Quinn leads the group in "metabolics," a workout where the work-to-rest ratio mimics that of game play; as the lockout grew longer, the sets and reps did as well. By the end of the summer, the players were doing four quarters of fifteen plays (sixty plays) with 25–40 seconds of rest after each play. These guys were prepared once training camp started!

Brian Dawkins addresses the group on the developments of the lockout. Each week either Russ Hochstein or Dawkins would update the group and Landow where things stood and what the variable timetables were looking like. More than forty-five participants were in attendance on this particular day.

Joe Mays provides some comic relief during the lockout. Joe Mays had LaMar's Donuts delivered to the field after the last off-season workout. Although not the ideal post-workout nourishment, everyone had a good laugh.

Eddie Royal and Matt Willis recover after the conditioning test while New York Giants' Derrick Martin thinks about diving into the doughnuts after the last workout.

Julius Thomas, Judianne Atencio, Cassius Vaughn, and Joe Mays pose for a picture after the last workout of the lockout. Judianne was instrumental in providing water, sports drinks, and lunches during the entire workout.

And it's not even a mental decision. It's a subconscious decision on what they're going to use when they break to cover a receiver, or an offensive player. I wanted to show different players how inefficient they were."

The initial workouts were heavy on footwork, coordination, and transitional movements into acceleration. There would be box drills, exercises that worked on a player's overall agility.

Landow's workouts feature quick-burst, high-intensity drills; then, give the athlete a minute break.

Then go again for not even five minutes. This was football he was training for, not a marathon.

Said Landow: "You have to look at the demands of the sport. In football we have an average of four to five seconds per play. When you're working four to five seconds per play, we're using a predominant energy system. A specific fuel. In that five seconds we're using what's called ATP-PC."

Knowshon Moreno, Brady Quinn, and Zac Robinson (QB Detroit Lions) consume the final sprint of the conditioning test, 300 shuttle.

Wait a minute, Loren. Slow down. ATP-PC?

"Adenosine triphosphate (ATP) in the phosphagen system. It's very specific to duration of work and intensity of work. The problem is, most coaches work outside the energy demands of the sport. So in football I know I've got 5 seconds of work, 40 seconds down, and it's repeated in a drive anywhere between three and twelve to fifteen plays. Or in a game, anywhere between sixty and seventy plays on your side of the ball. So even though football is played in a duration of a three-hour game, it's segmented into a series of 5-second plays with 40-second rests."

Working out for three hours, in other words, can be counterproductive to becoming physically and mentally ready for a three-hour game. Said Landow:

> There's timeouts, there's injury, there's time of possession. There's a lot of things that ultimately will change some of those rest patterns. On the flip side, there are no huddle offenses, two-minute drills that can ultimately change that normal work to rest pattern. But if you're not preparing guys for a high-speed effort within their reps, you're not preparing them to play their game. If you've been conditioning them for long, slow speeds, you're going to set them on the highway with a Moped, asking them to merge onto a 65-mile-an-hour highway at 25 miles an hour.

Truth is, most training programs hurt speed. Joe Mays really added burst. The Broncos' brass would never admit to this, but their intention from late-April on was to start Nate Irving, a third-round rookie from North Carolina State, at middle linebacker. If not right away, eventually during the 2011 season.

The kid never got his chance. Joe Mays kept Irving off the field, other than on special teams. When the 2011 season was finished, the Broncos re-signed Mays to a three-year, $12-million contract that included a 2012 guarantee of $4 million.

Teams don't pay that kind of money to a player with the idea of having him watch from the sidelines. Mays is now the Broncos' unquestioned middle linebacker—the first time since Al Wilson was forced to retire with a neck injury after the 2006 season that the team had the same "Mike" in back-to-back years.

Acceleration Progression Drills

The following progressions should be spread out over the course of six weeks with no more than two sessions per week. Err on the side of more recovery. Remember, this is technique-based work, not conditioning.

Wall drill (stance). Hold a leaning position of 60 degrees. Alignment from ear to ankle, with core braced and shoulders down and back. Weight on ball of foot. Hold for 15 seconds and repeat for 3 sets.

Wall drill (1 count). Hold a leaning position of 60 degrees. Alignment from ear to ankle, with core braced and shoulders down and back. One leg in punch position so shins are parallel with raised foot dorsi-flexed. On clap, quickly drive the raised leg to the down position while quickly punching the down leg to the loaded position. Only drive the legs with as much speed as you can control the body position. Repeat for 5 reps per leg. Rest 90 seconds and repeat for 3 total sets.

Wall drill (2 count). Hold a leaning position of 60 degrees. Alignment from ear to ankle, with core braced and shoulders down and back. One leg in the punch position so shins are parallel with raised foot dorsi-flexed. On clap, quickly drive the raised leg to the down position while quickly punching the down leg to the loaded position and just as quickly repeat the same punch-drive action. Repeat for 5 reps per leg. Rest 90 seconds and repeat for 3 total sets.

Wall drill (3 count). Hold a leaning position of 60 degrees. Alignment from ear to ankle, with core braced and shoulders down and back. One leg in the punch position so shins are parallel with the raised foot dorsi-flexed. On clap, quickly drive the legs in a punch-drive action for three total contacts. Repeat for 3–5 reps per leg. Rest 90 seconds and repeat for 2–3 sets.

Wall drill (rapid fire). Hold a leaning position of 60 degrees. Alignment from ear to ankle, with core braced and shoulders down and back. One leg in the punch position so shins are parallel with the raised foot dorsi-flexed. On clap, quickly punch and drive the legs until the next clap, then pause. Wait for clap and resume the punch-drive action until one more clap. No more than 5 seconds on each. Repeat for 3–5 seconds each. Rest 90 seconds and repeat for 2 sets.

Partner-resisted march. Leaning toward the ground with alignment of ear to ankle. Start with a punch-drive marching action, and as the punch occurs, both shins should be parallel with the raised foot dorsi-flexed. Keeping core braced, drive back behind the hips on the ball of the foot, drive the arms back leading with the elbow at roughly 90 degree angle. Maintain marching tempo for 10 yards while keeping alignment from ear to ankle. Rest 90 seconds and repeat for 3 sets.

Partner-resisted A run. Lean toward the ground with alignment from ear to ankle. With a running tempo while creating the same mechanics as the march, punch-drive with a faster and rhythmic tempo. The goal is not to pull the resistor but to use the resistance to maintain a constant lean angle. Drive the arms back leading with the elbow at roughly 90 degree angle. Punch drive for 5–10 yards while keeping alignment from ear to ankle. Rest 2 minutes and repeat for 3 sets.

Red Rocks

"Loren definitely helped me improve my game," Mays said. "He had me focus on certain things as far as running, the little things, the attention to detail that I had not been focusing on. He had you work on mechanical things when you're running that helped you get from point A to point B quicker."

There are only so many speeches a performance coach can deliver to keep his athletes motivated to work out through the grind of summer.

Landow needed more. He needed to mix it up. And he knew just the place. In June and July, Landow dedicated Thursdays to the Red Rocks Amphitheater in Morrison, Colorado.

The place is nationally known for its concerts. The Beatles once played there. The Grateful Dead sold out countless shows.

It may be the most beautiful setting in the world for a concert, and it would now be part of the Broncos' off-season training.

Joe Mays shows a quick transition to acceleration as he works on his closing speed.

Nestled in Red Rocks park is a 9,450-seat open-air arena that has been carved out from red sandstone rock that is estimated at 70 million years old. Give or take.

What can be seen in the background is a panoramic view of Denver. What can be felt is the 6,200 feet of altitude. The views, and the workouts, will take your breath away.

This may sound odd, but Broncos players came to both dread and welcome Red Rocks Thursdays. The players knew they were in for a gut-ripping, lung-bursting, body-collapsing workout.

Yet, wouldn't you know about professional athletes, Camp Dawkins-turned-Camp Landow always drew its highest attendance on Red Rocks Thursdays.

Why? One word: COMPETITION! Competition and, yes, maybe some pride. These are elite athletes. Red Rocks was the most challenging of workouts.

Skip Red Rocks? Be prepared to get dogged the next time you show up. Red Rocks became a badge of honor for these Broncos players.

Said Landow:

The workout intent was two-fold from my perspective. One, burst of acceleration and speed to begin. Two, by the end of the workout, lactate threshold training, meaning the athletes would train at a volume and intensity level that produced a training by-product called lactic acid.

The same heavy breathing and heavy burning leg feeling a player gets during a long, fourth-quarter drive—when lactate levels become high enough that sometimes throwing up becomes the body's way to deal with the high acidic levels.

To be clear, the intent was NOT to make the athletes puke. It was [to] build enough workload on them so that they could tolerate and postpone the rate of lactate threshold.

In other words, Landow added, "If you want to be tolerant to snakebite, we must give the athletes doses of venom."

The grueling nature of the Red Rocks workouts was a bit tricky for Landow. Again, he was building tolerance in a progressive manner and not just throwing darts blindfolded, hoping to hit a target—the lockout's conclusion—even though the target was unknown and moving.

The Red Rocks Workout

1. The players would run the theater seats, not the steps. This meant one yard of distance on each stride. There was a purpose behind this. By running the seats instead of the steps, it maximized power and mechanics of the hips to generate power.

2. In the initial set, the players would run ten rows of acceleration, then walk down. This high-effort attack was to simulate the acceleration burst of football. Five reps of ten rows in the first set.

3. After the first set, the players would rest for two to three minutes.

4. In the second set, the players would sprint up twenty rows of seats. Remember, running from seat to seat adding a full yard more to the stride than step to step. Five reps of twenty rows. This is when the altitude would start to become noticeable, and the guys who hadn't been working out would start to labor.

5. The rest was a little greater after these five reps as Landow wanted to prolong lactate accumulation. So the rest would be for about three to five minutes.

6. Set three. Getting tired, yet? This set separated the men from the boys. This set required the players to sprint up thirty rows. Five reps of thirty-row, incline sprints. The legs were now barking. Getting heavy. It was in this set that some players needed to take a seat and watch the others. At the start of each Red Rocks session, Landow would tell the players to stay within their limits. Oh, what competition does for these guys. There is no greater motivation than competition. The fear of losing. The feeling

of throwing up, on the other hand, can humble the greatest of competitors.

7. After five reps of thirty rows, the rest intervals went to five minutes.

8. Set four. Yes, there was a fourth set. This was the gut check: forty rows. Sprint up forty rows of seats. Three reps of forty rows.

9. Five-minute rest.

10. Set five. The parameters had been set to run as far as a player could with precise mechanics. That was the key—sprinting while holding the sprinter's mechanics. When the mechanics fail, the players were told to revert to a skip. Skip? The skip is a better biomechanical position than an exhausted sprint mechanics. Working hard was one objective. Working right was tied for the first objective.

There would be the occasional dropout at this point, but not many. Roughly 90 percent of the attendees were up for the final test. The final set. The final rep. The final sprint up those famous amphitheater seats.

After a five-minute rest came:

11. The finisher.

One time, the players had to start from the bottom and race up all seventy steps to the top, without stopping. If needed, the players could transition to the skip. Remember how set three started to separate the men from the boys? The finisher separated the athletes from the trainer.

Said Landow: "I would participate in the Red Rocks workouts and knowing myself, I knew there was a greater chance of me passing out before throwing up. Sure enough, I passed out! After five Red Rocks workouts, I knew what kind of shape these guys were in. Everyone from the 190-pounders to the 320-pounders were finishing the workouts, and not just finishing, but powering through them."

Landow, though, had understood his limits. He was not a Broncos player. He was a performance coach who trained the Broncos, while nobody was watching.

Loren Landow, passing out, with Bo Scaife, Ryan Harris, Ben Garland, Mitch Unrein, and Jeff Byers.

players would come and go. It was the off-season. Lockout or no lockout, it was a time when players would take family vacations, spend a long weekend with their college buddies, head back to their respective hometowns for four or five days to catch up with the folks and their friends.

Kuper and Russ Hochstein, veteran offensive linemen that they were, weren't around during the highly publicized early sessions of Camp Dawkins. For Kuper, who had been working out with Landow since before his scouting combine in 2006, it was only before and after the cameras stopped shooting that he carried on with his routine.

Fullback Spencer Larsen and punter Britton Colquitt also joined the team-organized workouts.

As some players stepped in, others took off on their scheduled down times. As Camp Dawkins was getting ready to shift from the Sports Dome to the outdoors in June, when the workouts took advantage of Colorado's beautiful summer mornings at Valor Christian High School, Dawkins himself traded his role as team captain for that of father and husband.

The names didn't matter to Landow. Whether it was Brian Dawkins or Braxton Kelly, Kevin Vickerson or Mitch Unrein, Landow felt responsible for their overall well-being as Broncos players.

Besides, the team workouts were becoming self-sufficient, anyhow. It took a leader the caliber of Dawkins to get it started, but once the routine was established, the Broncos-only workout became more Camp Landow. Camp Broncos.

"We have been doing workouts that have a lot of movement," said cornerback Cassius Vaughn. "The best thing about this is, we're together as a team. It's a bunch of guys that want to work. It's a time of year where a lot of what you enjoy is being around your teammates."

In all, roughly thirty-five Broncos attended the team workouts during the lockout summer of 2011. The sporadic attendance challenged Landow. A player he had been training for two months might require a different workout than a player who was showing up for the first time.

But the foundation of each workout, the principles behind them, applied to all players at various stages of their fitness.

Said Landow: "Whether I had them for one week or three months, I had to prepare them to play the game on a physiological level. What I said from day one was, 'I'm not here to strategize Xs and Os. I'm here to get them ready for when the lights go back on.'"

On July 1, the Friday of the holiday weekend, Camp Dawkins concluded. Dawkins was no longer participating in the team workouts. As a safety about to enter his sixteenth year in the NFL, he understood that the "off" part of an off-season must not be dismissed. Players have to recharge. A husband and father of four young children, Dawkins took time with his family. He was also heavily involved in the labor negotiations as the Broncos' primary union rep.

In truth, the Broncos' workouts didn't so much dissolve as they merged. Landow had been directing two NFL-oriented workouts a day, four days a week, since May 10.

The first session consisted of local NFL players (such as John Matthews and Kasey Studdard), locally based NFL free agents (Bo Scaife, Justin Bannan, Demetrin Veal, Jesse Nading, Cole Pember-ton, and Shelley Smith) and college free agents (Colorado School of Mines defensive lineman Marc Schiechl).

The second session consisted of Broncos players. As of July 5 and until further notice, Landow combined his two groups into one morning session. The Broncos had been working out at the Sports Dome down the road from team headquarters in Engle-wood until moving to Highlands Ranch in late June to mix in with Ed McCaffrey's football camp at Valor Christian High.

Landow had forty-five to fifty players at his combined session on July 5 at Valor Christian. Tebow was one of the Broncos who worked out with the likes of Schiechl. In other words, Broncos players would continue to work out; they just didn't get their pri-vate session with Landow.

"I absolutely believe it served its purpose as far as building camaraderie and competition among the teammates," Landow said on July 5 in tying a bow on Camp Dawkins. "One reason why we decided to go to one group for now is so we could continue to build on the competition. Going forward, we'll make adjustments depending on what happens (with labor negotiations) in the next ten days or so."

On the same day Landow held his first combined session at Valor Christian High, negotiators representing the owners and players resumed talks in New York City. They met for three days, and then on July 8, an appeals court in St. Louis struck the players a blow by saying the lockout was a legal negotiating tactic.

The court ruling gave the owners much-needed leverage and

motivated the players' side to make a deal before training camp was scheduled to begin. And camp was scheduled to begin in—gulp—two weeks.

One day, multiple reports said a labor settlement was imminent. The players believed these reports were leaked from the owners' side. The next day, the players would send word that any report of imminent resolution was premature.

"Looking at it from a business side of it, you know things don't get done months before they're supposed to or until there's deadlines," Kuper said. "But I was a little worried towards the end when the media got involved, and you hear different stories from each media outlet. So we tried to get to the bottom of it. Russ was there and Russ was our union guy, or Dawkins, and we'd get the real story. But it wasn't an everyday thing. Maybe towards the end when you weren't sure when we were coming back."

Whatever the reality, the players' biological clocks were wound tight. There was a different feel to Landow's workouts in the month of July.

The dog days of June were replaced by the giddyup of July. Maybe it was the great Colorado outdoors. Maybe it was the optimistic belief that somehow, someway, the owners and player leaders would find common ground. Or maybe it was the time of year when even the laziest of NFL players instinctively knows it's time to roll up the bag of potato chips and get up off the couch.

Whatever the reason, more players showed up at Landow's workouts, anxious to get ready. The intensity of the workouts picked up. There was far more chatter and camaraderie among players following the workouts.

Even though the Broncos-organized workouts halted on July 1, in many ways July was the month when Landow's workouts solidified the team that would become that year's AFC West champions.

CHAPTER 7

Brady Quinn Leads till the End

THE BRONCOS would not have won the AFC West title if not for their two-minute drill.

They were down 15–0 at Miami on October 23 when they scored on hurry-up drives of 80 yards and 56 yards in the final five minutes to win 18–15 in overtime.

The Broncos would have failed to reach the play-offs for a sixth consecutive season had they not executed their two-minute drill to beat the New York Jets on Thursday night November 17 in prime time. Or the San Diego Chargers on November 27. Or the Minnesota Vikings on December 4. Or the Chicago Bears on December 11.

And when did the Broncos first start working on their two-minute drill that won them so many games? In July, when nobody was watching.

It was on a nondescript soccer field, located just off the magnificent football stadium at Valor Christian High School, that Brady Quinn would gather his teammates, organize the receivers, and motivate the five linemen into at least repeating dry runs of two-minute drill plays.

Brady Quinn is proof that a player doesn't have to play in order to contribute.

"One hundred percent true," said Landow. "Midway through our camp, Brady would say: 'Hey, Loren's working with us, but here's what I'm going to do with the guys after he's done.'

"I'm sure there were some guys who disliked it when after a hard workout, Brady would pull them in and say, 'OK, we're going to do the two-minute drill.' He would make them run it at high tempo and talk to them about protections. I would say he took on, for lack of a better term, a coaching role. It was a coaching-player role."

The theater and drama industry understand that it's not just the actors who are key to a performance's success. It is why after every movie, credits are rolled to recognize the dozens, if not hundreds, of people who contribute behind the scenes. The makeup people, key grip, boom operator, wardrobe, sound, lighting.

Quinn was an essential backstage contributor to the Broncos' success in 2011.

A former star quarterback at Notre Dame, Quinn was a first-round draft pick, number 22 overall, of the Cleveland Browns in 2007, but his professional career quickly became a series of tough breaks.

As a rookie, Quinn played well in the preseason, but 2007 was the year—the only year—that journeyman veteran Derek Anderson put it all together and had a Pro Bowl season.

Quinn got his chance to start midway through the 2008 season, but after an impressive start against the Broncos, throwing for two touchdowns and no interceptions while posting a 104.3 passer rating, he broke the index finger of his right (passing) hand in his second start, an injury that eventually led to the season-ending injured reserve list.

Quinn was again the starter for a horrific Browns team in

2009 and was sensational in game 10 at Detroit, completing 21 of 33 passes for 304 yards, four touchdowns, no picks, and a 133.1 rating. That was the first of four games Quinn played without throwing an interception, but the streak ended in game 14 against the Kansas City Chiefs when he suffered a season-ending broken foot.

If Brady Quinn didn't get a break, he'd get no break at all.

The subsequent off-season brought an overhaul in Browns' management, and the new man in charge, Mike Holmgren, wanted to move on from Quinn. Holmgren felt Quinn's enormous popularity in Cleveland could be a distraction. A native of Dublin, Ohio, the handsome quarterback had a near Tebow-like following in Cleveland.

So Quinn was traded March 14, 2010, to the Broncos, where new coach Josh McDaniels was an offensive coordinator disciple of Charlie Weis, Quinn's head coach at Notre Dame.

The trade to Denver and coach McDaniels were extremely promising to Quinn. Six weeks later, the impetuous McDaniels fell in love with a quarterback prospect named Tim Tebow; and after the former Heisman Trophy winner and two-time national champion from Florida became the number 25 overall pick in the 2010 draft, Quinn's opportunity with the Broncos was doomed before he started.

McDaniels would change his mind again, this time focusing his affection on Orton, who was given a two-year contract extension in training camp. Orton played at a Pro Bowl level in the first ten games of the 2010 season, but after the team went so far south that McDaniels was fired with four games remaining, interim head coach Eric Studesville and general manager Brian Xanders thought it would be best for the franchise's long-term planning if they gave Tebow a season-ending audition.

Still, Quinn never surrendered. Even though he never took a snap during the 2010 season, Quinn worked intently during the off-season with quarterbacks coach David Lee. He was with Lee in

Fort Lauderdale, Florida, through most of the month of May, when Camp Dawkins was in its formative stages.

"When I heard about what Brian was doing with the workouts, I wanted to come out to see how the workouts were," said Quinn, himself a highly trained athlete. "I think I came out a couple times in May. And I enjoyed my time working with Loren. I really liked him. I thought he was incredibly innovative and intelligent, and he was well beyond what other people were doing. So I worked with him from afar until I came back in June."

What exactly did Quinn mean when he said Landow was innovative? Was it extensive warm-up sessions? The specific way the workout mimicked the movements of a particular football position? The way Landow had his athletes take off their shoes and go barefoot during the five-minute cooldown?

"It was all of that," Quinn said. "The barefoot stuff, realizing that you need that sort of proprioception in order to build strength in the small muscles of the feet and create stability—I think you need to do that as much as possible, and he gets that."

(Proprioception is the awareness of posture, movement, and, in this case, knowledge of positioning, weight, and resistance as they relate to the body.)

Single-Leg Low-Amplitude Hops Barefoot

The goal of the barefoot series is to strengthen the intrinsics of the foot and ankle. If we want athletes to be tolerant of snakebite (injury), they need to be given doses of venom (progressions of training stress). The stronger and more stable the foot and ankle are, the faster and healthier the athlete can be. In teaching the foot to have eccentric control, or stopping strength, the less torque we create at the knee each time the foot hits the ground on a jump, sprint, or change of direction, the better. That said, the stronger the foot, the better the platform we have to produce force into the ground with less waste.

The following progression should not be considered the goal, but more how it is being completed. How stable and controlled the athlete performs the drill is the objective. Again, it is not about how far the athlete hops but how well he lands. The athlete needs to have single-leg competency with force absorption before moving on to the next progression.

1-count hop stick. Standing on one leg with a slight knee bend (10–20 degrees). Hop sub-maximal at a 45-degree angle, while keeping the core braced, and neutral alignment of knee, hip, and shoulders. Land full-footed with slight knee bend (10–20 degrees) and minimize any further movement from the hips, trunk, and shoulders on landing (slight double hop is preferred instead of altering body position for balance). Once at a complete stop, hop at a 45-degree angle the other direction, landing on the opposite leg, full-footed landing with minimal movement on landing from the knee, hips, trunk, and shoulder. 5–8 reps each leg; rest 90 seconds.

2-count hop stick. Standing on one leg with slight knee bend (10–20 degrees). Hop sub-maximal at a 45-degree angle, while keeping the core braced, and neutral alignment of the knee, hip, and shoulders. Upon landing, quickly bound 45 degrees the other direction and stick the landing on the same leg full-footed with the knee bend at 10–20 degrees. 5–8 reps; rest for 60 seconds and then perform the drill with the other leg leading.

"And then when you look at his warm-up," Quinn continued, "it's dynamic, but it allows the whole entire body to turn itself on and you're going to be activating all muscles we're going to be using while working out.

"And, then, when you go into his workout, everything is created to target specific purposes with specific drills. A lot of it he tries to simulate to what we're going to do out there on the field. Which is the best scenario."

Although Quinn did not participate in the Camp Dawkins workouts in May, he went back to Florida as a Landow client. Like so many of Landow's long-distance customers, Quinn used workouts Landow devised for him over the phone.

3-count hop stick. Standing on one leg with slight knee bend (10–20 degrees). Hop sub-maximal at a 45-degree angle, while keeping the core braced, and neutral alignment of the knee, hip, and shoulders. Upon landing, quickly bound 45 degrees the other direction and then quickly rebound one more time 45 degrees back again and stick the landing full-footed with the knee bend at 10–20 degrees. 5–8 reps; rest for 90 seconds.

On June 14, Quinn worked out with the Broncos for the first time.

He immediately looked like a much-improved quarterback. To begin his off-season, Quinn first sought counsel from longtime NFL and college offensive coordinator Paul Hackett. They looked at film of Quinn's rookie year, which included a splendid pre-season debut against the Broncos.

Then they looked at film of Quinn's second year, 2008, when he made an impressive starting regular-season debut, again against the Broncos.

Then they looked at his third year, when Quinn's career moved beyond stalled and into a full-blown struggle.

5-count hop stick. Standing on one leg with slight knee bend (10–20 degrees). Hop sub-maximal at a 45-degree angle, while keeping the core braced, and neutral alignment of the knee, hip, and shoulders. Rebound at a 45-degree angle and stick full-footed on the fifth contact with knee bend at 10–20 degrees while minimizing movement from the knee, hip, trunk, and shoulders. 4 reps; rest 90 seconds.

First, Hackett worked on the person. He told Quinn to take time away from football. Play golf. Watch a baseball game. Spend time with kids.

When a player feels good about himself, he grows as a player. Quinn then went to Coach Lee, whose passing sessions emphasized footwork. Quinn was noticeably sharper with his throws on the first day at Landow's workout. He threw with considerable zip as he put the ball in the chest of receivers running seam routes, and in the eye-level hands of pass catchers on the sidelines.

His confidence bolstered, Quinn's mind was free.

"I want to be number one," Quinn told the *Denver Post* that day. "I feel they (Orton and Tebow) both had a chance last year, and I didn't get an opportunity. I'd love to get an opportunity to help us win games and get this team to the play-offs and see what happens from there."

Quinn would be the best of the Broncos' three quarterbacks through the first two preseason games, but another season would go by without taking one snap. Orton was already entrenched as the starter, and Tebow was the quarterback who got the nod after the Broncos started 1–4.

Not that Quinn wasn't part of a Broncos team that would reach the postseason for the first time in six years.

Quinn started attending the Landow-led Broncos' workouts in mid-June, in part because he wanted to get in some altitude conditioning. About the time Quinn became a regular participant in Camp Dawkins, the camp's namesake started taking some personal time with his family.

Dawkins has a wife, Connie, and four children. A man has to give his family time. If not in late-June and the first-half of July, when?

There is no other time. Family, in terms of time, takes a backseat once training camp starts in late-July.

"Guys did one of two things in July," Quinn said. "When it got close, guys either turned up the intensity, knowing it was close. Or they were: I better get a couple days off, because once it starts we're going full go, there is no more downtime."

Landow couldn't worry about the guys who weren't there. His concern was for those who did attend his sessions. As for what Landow thought would be the best for the Broncos, he made the strategic decision to consolidate his two football groups for the month of July.

Camp Dawkins had moved outside, from the Sports Dome to Valor Christian High School in the final week of June, because

Landow was also committed to working with kids at the Ed McCaffrey football camp.

Landow put in an exhausting schedule. He would work with two NFL football groups in the morning on a field just off Valor's football stadium, then he would join McCaffrey on the stadium field to work with kids in the afternoon.

And that week, it was scorching hot in the Denver area. Landow's first morning session consisted of local NFL players (such as John Matthews and Kasey Studdard), locally based NFL free agents (Bo Scaife and Justin Bannan), and college free agents (Colorado School of Mines defensive lineman Marc Schiechl).

His second morning session consisted of players on the Broncos' current roster.

Reducing his workload, though, wasn't the reason Landow consolidated his two NFL groups. The reasons were, one, he wanted to increase the competition for the Broncos players; and, two, he needed enough receivers and defenders for Quinn to run his post-workout, passing, and two-minute drill sessions.

The final day of Camp Dawkins was July 1, the Friday before the holiday weekend. The Broncos were typically drawing twelve to fifteen players to each of Landow's workout sessions. Merging groups would mean more players participating in drills, which, in turn, would raise the competition within those drills.

On Tuesday, July 5, Landow had forty-five to fifty players at his combined session at Valor. The players at that first combined session ranged from Tebow, who popped in and out of Denver throughout the summer, to Dain Taylor, a pass-rushing defensive end/outside linebacker from Mountain Vista High School in Highlands Ranch and Drake University who would be trying to catch on with an NFL team as an undrafted rookie once the lockout ended.

Thanks to Landow, the Broncos had a chance to train right up until the NFL said "go." And "go" would be the word once the lockout was resolved with a new collective bargaining agreement.

Eric Decker works on acceleration A runs with Matt Willis providing resistance. Eddie Royal warms up in the background.

Said Landow on the challenges of administering the proper workout during the month of July: "Every week it was always like: 'We'll see where the lockout is at the end of the week and then we'll start with the appropriate workout on Monday.' If we went into the weekend without a deal getting done, I would increase their volume on Monday and Tuesday, and then Thursday and Friday I'd start peeling it back significantly, so that way, if a deal was struck over the weekend, they could walk into a Monday workout recovered."

Athletes get into start position for "metabolics" or conditioning that specifically mimics the demands of the sport.

Athletes set in "ready" position as Landow is about to start the drill on his verbal command.

Athletes shuffle and decelerate, repeating similar patterns of work for four sets of twenty plays with 25–40 seconds of rest between plays and 3 minutes of recovery between sets.

This is fact: The Broncos were the only team who continued to work out as a group until the day the lockout ended. Alex Smith and the San Francisco 49ers ended their player workouts on July 1. Other teams also used the long holiday weekend to break for some R & R. Still other teams only had their players gather for a couple weeks, and some never did organize player workouts.

The first three weeks of July is normally the time when players take a vacation before training camp begins in late-July.

At Valor Christian High School in Highlands Ranch, though, Quinn used those three weeks to galvanize the group.

Mostly through texting, Quinn would recruit receivers Matt Willis and Eric Decker to come run routes after Landow's workout. Demaryius Thomas was coming off Achilles surgery, so he wasn't available. Eddie Royal attended a few sessions in July, but he was lightly coming back from hip surgery. Brandon Lloyd was doing his own thing.

That only gave Quinn a small group of receivers to work with. He called in some tight ends, Dan Gronkowski and Richard Quinn. Fourth-round rookie tight end Julius Thomas took the initiative to cold-call Quinn and stay at the veteran quarterback's condo for a couple of weeks. Running back Lance Ball deserved a camp award for his regular attendance—and unpretentious willingness to help Judianne Atencio load the water coolers into her vehicle.

But Quinn—more subtly than demonstratively—became the player others looked to.

"I think for those young receivers, Brady became their leader during the lockout," said Chris Kuper. "He was the only quarterback out there."

Said Quinn: "In all fairness to Brian (Dawkins), he's an older player so he needed to rest his body as much as he can. I got the sense there was an opportunity there to step up and take a leadership role. I didn't really care if the coaches saw it or not. I wanted the players to see how I felt about them."

And it wasn't just during the morning workouts at Valor. On Monday, July 11, Quinn and Landow rounded up the guys for a group trip to the Children's Hospital Colorado on the Anschutz Medical Campus in Aurora.

As Mike Klis wrote in the *Denver Post*:

The world today can be harshly critical with bloggers, tweeters and reporters constantly talking about what a football player can't do.

How about what these guys can do? What an NFL player contingent led by Quinn and their personal trainer Loren Landow did Monday was lighten the moods of several kids fatigued from fighting off serious illness. The football group also included Russ Hochstein, Tyler Polumbus (whose foundation makes him a frequent visitor to Children's), Erik Pears, Seth

Loren and Lance Ball have a laugh between drills.

Olsen, Braxton Kelly, and undrafted free agents Chad Friehauf, Ryan Echer, and Augustine Agyei.

Quinn, Landow, and punter Britton Colquitt visited with Olivia Current of Longmont who is blond, beautiful, 16, and was diagnosed June 30 with acute myeloid leukemia, and Rileigh Adams, 12 of Colorado Springs, a cutup with the most humorous facial expressions, and bald after receiving a bone marrow transplant on June 2.

"How many books have you read?" Colquitt asked Rileigh.

It turns out Rileigh is a voracious reader. The best guesstimate by her mom is she has read about 20 books a year for the past six or seven years.

"So, you've read more books in one year than I have in my life," Colquitt said.

Olivia's leukemia is treatable and curable. Her most recent cell count reading was extremely encouraging. Then she got a visit from the Broncos and a conversation with Quinn.

"That was cool," said Olivia's father Joe Current. "Everyone is still buzzing. The whole room was buzzing after they left."

Better believe the players get something out of these visits, too.

"I remember when I was in sixth grade, I played in a travel football league," Quinn said. "We got our butts kicked every single game. I thought life was rough just because we lost football games. You come in here even for one day and you see how these kids have been hit with life-threatening illnesses. It makes us realize how fortunate we are to be in the position we're in."

The lockout was down to its final week. On Wednesday, July 19, Dawkins was in Washington, D.C., as the Broncos' union rep going over the collective bargaining agreement proposal that the owners had presented and player union chief DeMaurice Smith had agreed to in principle, if not in full detail.

The expectation was that the lockout would be lifted that Friday, and Broncos players would once again belong to the Broncos.

"I think a lot of guys are in disbelief," Quinn said then. "We've been hearing for a while now that we're close that I think guys are waiting to hear the word. It's been tough trying to anticipate things. As athletes, we live on anticipation. It's been where we've not been able to do that."

The previous day, on Tuesday, July 18, so many Broncos players had attended the Camp Landow workout session at Valor that Quinn had lined them up to run the two-minute offense.

J. D. Walton delivered shotgun snaps from center. Russ Hochstein, Zane Beadles, Chris Kuper, and Ryan Harris worked on their pass blocking steps with Jeff Byers and Chris Clark working in.

Tight ends Richard Quinn and Dan Gronkowski ran pass routes, as did receiver Matt Willis. Lance Ball blocked and ran routes from his tailback spot.

In all, eighteen Broncos players attended the conditioning workout that day. Besides the aforementioned offensive players, other Broncos who participated in the workout Tuesday were Robert Ayers, Joe Mays, Cassius Vaughn, Braxton Kelley, Kyle McCarthy, and Mitch Unrein.

Three days later, on Thursday, July 21, Brian Dawkins arrived back home from his duties on the labor front in Washington, D.C. Negotiations were picking up, and Dawkins, the team's player rep and a union board member, was heavily involved.

By happenstance, Dawkins arrived at Valor Christian High School to watch his son, Brian Jr., participate in his first freshman practice. While there, Dawkins glanced toward the other end of the field. Well, what do you know about that? He saw that the football players practicing on the other side of the field were Broncos!

The man who started it all, Brian Dawkins, had been away with his family and on players' union assignment for the past three weeks. He didn't realize so many guys were still working out with Landow.

Dawkins walked over to watch the final half of the workout, then he huddled the players to brief them on where negotiations stood with the owners: A deal was close, but there were still plenty of details to work out, and the issues were significant enough that it could blow up at any time. Be optimistic a new CBA will be worked out by early next week. But hang tight.

The next day, Friday, July 22, was Landow's last day with the Broncos as a group. Fittingly, Dawkins was there to work out with the guys.

The word that morning was that a labor resolution would come in time for the players to report to their teams on Monday. Landow took off on Friday for a family vacation to San Diego.

His work for all Broncos but Tebow and Quinn, who continued to work with Landow through the 2011 season, was done.

Said Landow: "As this thing dragged on, I figured there was too much money at stake in these preseason games that a deal was going to get done. And it did look like it would get done about the same time training camp was supposed to start."

He was happy to graduate his group. Landow was never in it to work with Broncos players day in, day out. He's worked with many great NFL players and athletes. Peter Forsberg. Chad Brown. Tom Nalen. Brian Griese. Gus Frerotte. Adam Foote. Joel Dreessen. Mike Anderson. Tyler Brayton. Domota Peko. Andy Levitre. Ed McCaffrey. Bo Scaife. Jeremy Bloom. Bill Romanowski. Missy Franklin. Alicia Sacramone. Kara Lynn Joyce. Bobby Brown.

Landow has been around too many stars to be starstruck. He was in this to get the Broncos in condition for training camp, to increase their odds of staying injury-free during the 2011 season, to help them build a championship while no one was watching.

And all that happened. Thanks in part to Landow. Thanks in part to Quinn. It may have been Tebow who executed all those final-minute thrills for the Broncos. But behind the scenes, Quinn's work with the two-minute drill in July no doubt helped Tebow's supporting cast.

"The two-minute, that's when you need to be mentally sharp," Quinn said. "That's when you have to perform the best. I don't know. Maybe it started in the summer. Maybe that helped some of those guys, whether it was Matt Willis or Decker or Lance Ball."

CHAPTER 8

Staying Healthy

I think we'll be a lot more bonded this year. Everybody knows each other a little more, because we all had to pull together and work out by ourselves and we all came together that way.

—Britton Colquitt, Broncos punter, on how the lockout
workouts with performance coach Loren Landow would
benefit the team in 2011

N THE FIRST WEEK of the 2011 training camp—which was also the last week of July—Broncos star linebacker D. J. Williams, who did not attend Camp Dawkins during the lockout, suffered a strained quad.

Williams missed most of the first two weeks of camp.

Broncos star pass rusher Elvis Dumervil, who like Williams spent the lockout training in his off-season home of Miami, suffered a strained groin and missed the final week of August.

Running back LenDale White, who showed up for the Camp

Dawkins Media Day session on May 13 but never again, was waived in training camp. Almost a full year after suffering a ruptured Achilles, White suffered back spasms that lingered a week before he was released. He never caught on with another team during the 2011 season.

Broncos receiver Brandon Lloyd, who showed up for one Camp Dawkins session but only to run routes and catch passes from quarterback Kyle Orton, tweaked his groin in the season-opening loss against the Oakland Raiders and missed the week two game against the Cincinnati Bengals.

The Broncos suffered other significant injuries to players who—coincidentally but probably not—did not train with Landow during the players-only workouts at the bubble or Valor Christian High School.

Demaryius Thomas, the Broncos' first-round drafted wide receiver in 2010, blew out his Achilles in February 2011 while working on a drill in Atlanta. The Broncos' two starting defensive tackles after their first preseason game at Dallas, Marcus Thomas and Ty Warren, each suffered strained muscles to their upper extremities. During the same morning practice of August 15, Thomas strained a pectoral muscle and missed the first four games of the season; and Warren blew out his triceps, an injury that forced the Broncos' top free agent to miss the entire season.

The Broncos still had to pay Warren a $4-million salary in 2011. It was another reminder of how the investment in proper off-season training can pay itself back millionfold.

Undrafted rookie cornerback Brandon Bing, who got a $3,000 bonus, strained his calf in camp and was cut. Meanwhile, cornerback Chris Harris, who only got a $2,000 bonus to sign with the Broncos, stayed healthy, made the team, and wound up becoming their number one nickel back, covering the likes of Wes Welker, the NFL's top pass catcher nearly every year, in late-season games against the New England Patriots.

Ask any player: The number one key to any season is staying

healthy. Once an athlete reaches the most elite level, it can be argued that injury prevention is right there with talent when it comes to whether that athlete makes it.

Has it been mentioned? Through training camp and the pre-season, none of the regular participants in the Brian Dawkins-organized workouts this off-season who were supervised by trainer Loren Landow suffered so much as a pulled hamstring.

"The stuff he teaches you about your body, as far as your flexibility—and then the drills that complement those that pertain to injury prevention—those are the most important things I take away from it," said right guard Chris Kuper, the senior member of the Broncos' offensive line. "Because I can condition myself and run as many 100s as I want. But having the correct amount of rest, getting your body fully warmed up—I can do a static stretch and run twelve 100s. But a warm-up with Loren is thirty-five to forty minutes on some days before we condition. He gets every part of the body warmed up, ready to go. I mean you didn't see anybody out there pulling muscles."

Loren cues Joe Mays through a dynamic flexibility exercise "leg cradle."

Nope. Not one soft-tissue injury from the Landow group through camp, preseason, and the regular season.

Compare the Landow soft-tissue report card in 2011 to the Broncos' 2010 training camp, when after a full off-season of team conditioning they lost their top two running backs, Knowshon Moreno and Correll Buckhalter, in the first hour of training camp. Dumervil, the NFL's defending sack champion, suffered a season-ending injury during the second of a two-a-day camp practice in early August of 2010.

Yet in the year of the lockout, the Broncos got out of training camp far healthier than they did in the second year of head coach Josh McDaniels. Among the reasons McDaniels failed as a head coach in Denver was that he underestimated the importance of the starting line.

To the contrary, Landow fretted so much about the starting line, there was reason to wonder if he wasn't *overestimating* the starting line.

Said Landow: "I was preparing them for a moving target, which was either an OTA, or was it actually for training camp? If it was training camp and the preseason, then I had to get these guys ready for a twenty-week car wreck. Which is what playing football is. I had to get their bodies tolerant to collisions, full-speed acceleration, and abrupt deceleration. For twenty weeks of the season there, your body is essentially going through a car accident."

One game into the 2011 season, injuries to the players who had not worked out with Landow during the lockout were threatening to kill the Broncos' play-off hopes.

It's difficult enough trying to win an NFL game with a full roster complement. Trying to win on Sunday with so many star players hobbled on the sidelines is almost impossible. It was getting so bad for the Broncos that their players were suffering injuries while recuperating from injuries.

The most bizarre and troubling case involved Marcus Thomas. He strained the right pectoral muscle during a training camp practice August 15. The pec, though, was coming around, and the Broncos had realistic hopes Thomas would be available to play in the season opener, September 12, against the rival Oakland Raiders.

But as Thomas was running sprints to get back in shape for the opener, he strained his groin. It was the groin strain, not the pec, that caused Thomas to miss the first four games of the season.

Although Landow's clients are not completely immune to a muscle pull, the odds are considerably less. It's hard to believe Thomas would have strained his groin had he warmed up the Landow way.

Landow on his warm-up:

It's a head-to-toe process of warming up the machine section by section. Meaning, I account for every joint range of motion in all the planes that the joint should move in. I don't advocate how much range of motion, but where is the range coming from and what is the strength through that range. All the while I monitor symmetry of segments from left to right.

We make sure we attack segments of the body in quadrants.

We'll do a full hip series, a full trunk series; we'll do an ankle, knee, and hip series where we're just working on an increase in range of motion while also basically providing an environment of stability at the same time.

And as the warm-up progresses, it becomes more dynamic. Not unlike what they will encounter in their sport, mimicking acceleration and deceleration and forcing the neuromuscular system great control during the eccentric phase of contraction. Again, we want to prepare the muscular system for what the demands of the sport will be.

Too bad the Broncos didn't have 100 percent attendance at Camp Dawkins. In that opener against the Raiders, a disappointing

23–20 loss that was played on a damp, chilly, fall night in Denver, cornerback Champ Bailey and running back Knowshon Moreno suffered torn hamstrings.

Two weeks into the regular season, the Broncos had ten projected starters miss at least one game because of injuries, five because of leg strains. The five: Bailey, Moreno, Brandon Lloyd, Marcus Thomas, and Eddie Royal. Only Royal worked out with Landow, and he didn't show up until the final week because the receiver/returner was coming off hip surgery.

Why were Landow's clients staying healthy while so many non-Landow clients were helplessly watching the Broncos' struggle?

"The first thing is, he's very educated on understanding how to get results out of athletes from a physical standpoint with his workouts, but also from a mental standpoint," said backup quarterback Brady Quinn. "He's very positive. He's very direct with getting a good feel for your body and what your body is telling you. And he's a coach who continually has a calm demeanor. Even though the intensity of the workouts are at the highest level, you still need to remind yourself to remain calm and poised."

Despite Landow's training, the Broncos started the season 1–4. At least that lone win was impressive. Even though the Broncos had ten projected starters sidelined because of injuries for game two against a Cincinnati Bengals team that would eventually make the play-offs, quarterback Kyle Orton and second-year receiver Eric Decker had big games, connecting for two touchdowns in a 24–22 win at Sports Authority Field at Mile High.

The victory did give the Broncos confidence going into game three at Tennessee against the tough, physical Titans. The Broncos had thoroughly outplayed Tennessee through three quarters. Not only were they leading 14–10 entering the fourth quarter, they had the ball first-and-goal at the Tennessee 2. Four plays later, though, the ball had only advanced to the 1.

Instead of scoring to go up 21–10 in the fourth, the Broncos wound up losing 17–14.

The shorthanded Broncos had fought gallantly, but when gallantry wasn't enough, the locker room was demoralized.

D. J. Williams and Champ Bailey were still out with injuries the following week, and the defending Super Bowl champion Green Bay Packers destroyed the Broncos' defense in a 49–23 rout.

Orton threw an early pick six that put the Broncos behind 14–3, then played well the rest of the first half. But as Packers quarterback Aaron Rodgers lit up the Broncos' secondary in the second half, even the Green Bay faithful were chanting, "We want Tebow!"

Orton's time as the Broncos' quarterback was down to minutes. By halftime of the following week's game against the AFC West rival San Diego Chargers at Sports Authority Field, the Broncos were losing at home, 23–13. And the score wouldn't have been that close had Broncos cornerback Cassius Vaughn not intercepted a Philip Rivers pass and returned it 55 yards for a touchdown.

The Chargers held the ball for more than 19 minutes of the 30-minute half. Orton played as if he had zero confidence. It seemed that playing the villain to Tebowmania had finally broken the veteran quarterback. Orton had completed six of thirteen passes for just 34 yards by halftime. As the Broncos were heading into their locker room for the 12-minute halftime break, Broncos head coach John Fox told his offensive coordinator Mike McCoy that he was switching quarterbacks.

McCoy ran alongside Tim Tebow on the way to the locker room and said, "Get ready. You're up."

Those words saved the season. That decision turned the Broncos from a team that seemed headed for another 4–12 season, into a team that would win the AFC West title.

Fox and McCoy may not have fully grasped how ready Tebow was. Tebow, you see, had been spending his Tuesdays off training one-on-one with Landow. Tebow was ready.

Tebow did not have instant success against the Chargers. His first two possessions were two three-and-outs, and the Broncos fell even further behind, 26–10, with 8:54 remaining in the game.

But that's when Tebow's game would establish another trend: When all seemed lost, when the clock ticked down to its final minutes, it became Tebow Time. He and running back Willis McGahee rammed the Broncos through the Chargers' defense for a touchdown march, Tebow himself scoring from 12 yards out. McGahee ran in the two-point conversion, and the Broncos had closed the score to 26–18.

Tebow would get the ball back and lead another touchdown drive. It was 26–24 Chargers with 3:19 remaining. Rivers led a final, and crucial, field goal drive that put San Diego up 29–24 with 24 seconds remaining and the Broncos 80 yards away from changing the outcome.

Tebow nearly pulled off the miracle. Two long completions moved the ball to the Chargers' 30 with 5 seconds remaining. With most of the country watching, Tebow scrambled and scrambled some more, and scrambled even more. Not only did the clock read 0:00, it read zero for several seconds.

His long throw into a crowded end zone was knocked down, incomplete.

Although the Broncos had lost, the sellout crowd at Sports Authority Field chanted: "Te-bow! Te-bow!"

Never had a loss felt so good.

Tebow then ran off an incredible string of victories. In his first start, October 23, at Miami, Tebow had completed just four of fourteen passes for 40 yards while taking five sacks for 27 yards of losses. That added up to 13 yards passing with three quarters, and all but 5 minutes and 23 seconds left in the fourth.

And then, from nowhere, Tebow got hot. Down 15–0, he threw two touchdown passes in the final 2:44 and ran in a two-point conversion to send the game into overtime. Broncos win.

Tebow and the Broncos were trounced by Detroit the following week, but then came a six-game winning streak. The Broncos didn't know it at the time, but they essentially clinched the AFC West after rallying to defeat the Chicago Bears, 13–10, in overtime in game 13.

The Broncos had three wins—against the Dolphins, the Chargers, and the Bears—in which they never led until the final play in overtime.

After beating the Bears, the Broncos were 8–5.

It was enough. Although the Broncos lost their final three games, they had the tiebreakers against San Diego and Oakland. The AFC West division belonged to the Broncos.

For the first time since the 2005 season, the Broncos were back in the play-offs.

Camp Dawkins had its payoff.

"I believe it did help," Dawkins said. "I knew how I wanted to work out. A lot of guys knew how they wanted to work out at home. But then you have guys who don't have that plan. And to have a venue for them to come and bond—and even when they're finished working out, finished running, they would go hang out together—that's a bond with each other. Especially the O-line. They would go hang out together a lot. They were the ones that were there the most. To build that bond, and that bond is seen by the other guys when they came in, it almost served like a magnet. It would pull more teammates into that bond. I know it's kind of crazy to understand it, but there was a positive energy that came from this."

Braxton Kelly, Karl Paymah, Robert Ayers, Loren Landow, and Joe Mays try to cool down after a 100-degree day with a tough metabolic session.

Indeed, when Camp Dawkins concluded its two months of Broncos players-only workouts on July 1, Landow was asked about the group's off-season performance.

"I was really impressed with the offensive linemen as a group," Landow told the *Denver Post*. "Their consistency and their gains in athleticism and fitness in a short amount of time was impressive."

Five of the Broncos' top seven offensive linemen were regular participants in Camp Dawkins, and, then, for the month of July, Camp Landow. Guards Zane Beadles, Chris Kuper, and Russ Hochstein; center J. D. Walton and "power" tackle/tight end Chris Clark. Beadles, Walton, and Kuper were starters. When Kuper went down in the regular-season final against Kansas City, Hochstein started the two play-off games.

Along the way, the Broncos went from averaging 86.8 yards rushing through the first four games to an NFL-best 190.4 rushing yards in the final twelve games.

Willis McGahee, who had averaged just 532 yards rushing in his previous three seasons with Baltimore, rushed for 1,199 yards as a thirty-year-old back behind the Broncos offensive line in 2011.

Said Landow: "The biggest thing that I saw from the O-line from my personal perspective was how quickly these guys were getting downfield. Seeing Zane Beadles, seeing Kuper, seeing J. D. Walton getting to that second level and throwing blocks."

It was Kuper who pulled the offensive linemen together. The offensive line wound up pulling in Dawkins. And Dawkins pulled in the Broncos.

"I thought it was great," Kuper said. "If there was any hesitation about paying, Dawkins took care of that. We had a place to

Judianne's car is filled with donated drinks from Powerade and Eldorado Springs and coolers filled with post-workout food.

Lateral view of metabolic workout.

work out, a good trainer to work us out. It was all for free. What Dawk did there was great. And then he had Judianne show up every day with water and take care of stuff; I think it made it easier on some of the young guys who were maybe teeter-tottering on whether to do it or not."

CHAPTER 9

Gone But Not Forgotten

O FULLY GRASP what a sports performance coach like Loren Landow can do for an NFL player, it helps to understand the comeback story of the Broncos' new tight end Joel Dreessen.

Having grown up a huge Broncos fan in Fort Morgan, a rural town of about 10,500 located eighty-five miles northeast of Denver, Dreessen played his college ball at Colorado State University in Fort Collins, then was selected in the sixth round of the 2005 NFL Draft by the New York Jets.

As a rookie, Dreessen played in fourteen games for head coach Herm Edwards and offensive coordinator Mike Heimerdinger, catching five passes and playing on most of the special teams.

All was going well for the Colorado kid.

But the Jets were so snakebit that year by a rash of quarterback injuries, they had to pull 42-year-old Vinny Testaverde out of retirement while also playing the likes of Brooks Bollinger and Kliff Kingsbury.

Valid as the QB injury excuse is to any team's failure, it could not save Edwards or his staff from losing their jobs. After the Jets finished 4–12, Edwards was replaced by Eric Mangini, a young defensive coordinator from the New England Patriots.

As Broncos fans well know from the brief but disappointing 2009–2010 era of Josh McDaniels, the "Patriots' Way" is not for everybody. Late in Mangini's first training camp of 2006, he cut Dreessen. Apparently, Dreessen didn't fit the "Patriot" type player that Mangini wanted to instill with the Jets.

The timing of his late release, and the fact that he played so much as a rookie, left Dreessen's career stuck between fourth and long and his own goalpost.

Strangely, the fourteen games he played as a rookie would work against Dreessen, because he was no longer eligible for practice squads. That meant teams couldn't carry him along for a few weeks until one of their 53-man roster spots opened up. And because Mangini didn't waive Dreessen until the final cut-down date, teams did not have openings on their just-filled 53-man rosters.

Bummed but far from resigned, Dreessen returned to Colorado so he could train with his favorite performance coach, Loren Landow. Landow's pre-combine training in January-February of 2005 helped Dreessen get drafted in April of that year. And now with his career at a crossroads, Dreessen would need Landow once again.

This can be a challenging time for Landow and his clients, but also a rewarding time for the coach. What millions of NFL fans don't realize is that the start of every regular season also means a trip to the unemployment line for hundreds of professional players.

The players in the area who don't give up chasing their dream call on Landow for help. In 2006, Dreessen joined the group of unemployed professional players who trained with Landow. Each week would begin with hope. Each week would end in disappointment.

"Every weekend, I'd be going to work out for a team," Dreessen said. "I had eight workouts during that season where I'd take a physical and workout. They'd all say the same thing: 'Man, you were impressive. We can't believe you're not on a team. But it's just not us right now.'"

And so, following his workout with team X, Dreessen would fly back to Colorado and continue training with Landow.

"We kind of stole the *Good Will Hunting* line," Dreessen said about the 1997 Academy Award-nominated movie. "He would say: 'My best days are going to be when you don't show up to work out here, anymore.'"

Landow continued to tweak Dreessen the athlete. He came up with drills, techniques that made Dreessen more explosive off the line of scrimmage, more fluid in his movements and route running, stronger at the point of attack.

Tight end is one of the most underappreciated positions in football, primarily because it's the most misunderstood. Fantasy players think the best tight ends are those with the most prolific receiving statistics. Inside the NFL industry, though, coaches and executives often value more the tight end who plays like a second left tackle.

Dreessen prides himself as a complete tight end. A tight end who can both block and catch.

But he needed Landow's help in his unemployed season of 2006 to get that way.

"He's seen guys like me so many times," Dreessen said of Landow. "Guys who had played in the league and are out and keep working out in case the opportunity comes. My year, everyone I was working out with, they were like, 'Damn, why is this guy still here?' I could tell. About halfway through 2006, I was thinking: 'These SOBs are thinking that about me. I'm going to prove them wrong.'"

Luckily for Dreessen, Landow is not only one of the country's foremost performance coaches; he's a pretty fair recruiter.

In 2005 and in the first four or five months of 2006, the Broncos had a young front-office executive named Rick Smith who would also occasionally work out with one of Landow's coaches at Velocity Sports Performance. At the same time, Landow was training Joel Dreessen.

It was easy to tell Smith was a bright, young executive who would go places, and, sure enough, that place was the Houston Texans. Smith became only the third African American general manager in NFL history when he assumed the Texans' top front-office position in June 2006.

He wasn't on the job for a month when he started hearing from Landow again about this tall, agile tight end named Dreessen.

"I talked to Rick often that year about other athletes," Landow said. "But I'd always mention in the course of that conversation, 'Hey, Rick, I'm telling you, you've got to take a look at this guy.'"

A couple of days after the Texans finished their 2006 season, Smith did sign Dreessen to what is called a future's contract.

Dreessen hasn't missed a game since.

A second-stringer and special teams player in 2007–2008, Dreessen became a starter midway through 2009 when the Texans' talented tight end Owen Daniels suffered a terrible, season-ending knee injury.

Dreessen finished the year with a career-high twenty-six catches and he beat that in 2010 with thirty-six receptions. Now used as almost a full-time starter along with Daniels, Dreessen caught six touchdown passes in 2011. When he became a free agent at season's end, he signed a three-year, $8.5-million deal with the Broncos, his favorite team as a kid.

A few years earlier, after he was pretty well established with Houston, Dreessen presented Landow with an autographed Texans' jersey. It read:

Loren,

Thank you for helping me start a career, thank you for helping me get it back.

Joel Dreessen

Dreessen runs at Red Rocks.

t was the first week of August 2011. Loren Landow had just returned from his family vacation in San Diego and he was suffering from withdrawal. And it wasn't the Pacific Ocean he was missing, spectacular as the sea is for someone who has grown up near the mountains.

It was when Landow returned from his much-needed respite and settled in back home that it hit him. The lockout was over. He would no longer be working out the Broncos.

Broncos players were back at training camp, running, blocking, popping, catching, throwing, and perspiring through the grind of NFL practice beneath the hot summer sun.

Said Landow:

I am used to that time of year, when the athletes leave me and they have to report to their teams for their conditioning tests and training camps. But this off-season was so long, I was relieved in one sense that the season was started, because I was busier than you know what. But there was also a huge void in my day. That time during the lockout kept me focused and kept me driven because day in and day out, I had to prepare these guys for a season when they didn't have any coaches. So, yeah, I did feel like something was missing for a while there.

Camp Dawkins may not have started until May 10, but truth is, Landow and several Broncos players, primarily the offensive linemen, got together six weeks before, in the final week of March.

The lockout was official on March 18. Chris Kuper, J. D. Walton, and Zane Beadles started working with Landow the next week.

They first gathered at the Big Bear Ice Arena, then moved to Sports Xcel, a warehouse-like structure in Englewood, Colorado, that was less than a mile away from the Dove Valley headquarters that Broncos players were forbidden to enter.

The idea was simple: If a 4–12 team works hard during the lockout, and a 12–4 team sits satisfied on its couch clicking channels and eating chips and dip, maybe the 4–12 team can catch up.

"I wish we had an agreement by now," Walton said on March 12, 2011. "But whenever they do tell us to go back, we have to be ready."

At the time, Broncos players were merged with other NFL players such as Justin Bannan, who the Broncos had just released to free agency but has since returned to the team; Demetrin Veal and Karl Paymah; locally raised NFL players such as Bo Scaife, John Matthews, and Kasey Studdard; and future rookies such as Nate Solder, Marc Schiechl, and Blaine Sumner.

A 300-pound mass of pure muscle, Bannan was seen shuffling like Muhammad Ali, then exploding into a sprint, running all the while with form.

Nate Solder (New England Patriots) works on lower-body power and stability with one exercise, medicine ball broad jumps.

John Matthews (Jacksonville Jaguars), Guy Miller, Zac Pauga, Shelly Smith (all Houston Texans) perform low ankle hops for stability and strength for the foot and ankle complex.

"What we do is we call it developing biomotor abilities," Landow said. "We want to work on speed, power, strength, flexibility, coordination. And working on all those we try to make a better athlete."

Landow trained one group of fifteen to eighteen players at 8 a.m. and the second at 9:30 a.m. Nothing like an early morning schedule to help instill discipline.

"I've been coming here since college," said Scaife, who played at Mullen High School and still lives with his family in Lone Tree even though he just played six seasons for the Tennessee Titans. "Loren's very detailed, and what I mean by detailed is every little aspect when it comes to competing on the football field, agility drills, injury prevention. Instead of just the basics—running to death and pumping iron—we're doing things that are football specific."

When the lockout ended in late July 2011, Scaife wound up where Dreessen was in 2006—out for the season but unretired. He went back to work with Landow.

Also like Dreessen, Scaife was counting on Landow for the second time in his career. Before he was through at the University of Texas, Scaife would have three ACL surgeries. The injuries led to a medical hardship that resulted in Scaife becoming a sixth-year senior for the Longhorns.

When he played and was healthy, he was productive. But the knee concerns had him rated by one draft website as the 27th-best tight end entering the 2005 draft. The Tennessee Titans made a low-risk, sixth-round investment in Scaife, and he made the team as a third-string tight end/special teams player.

By the end of his rookie season, Scaife had thirty-seven catches. Eventually, the Tennessee Titans placed the franchise tag on him—making him one of the highest paid tight ends in the NFL. A free agent during the lockout, Scaife caught on with the Cincinnati Bengals, but in the final preseason game he suffered a neck injury that required a cervical fusion to repair and was placed

Alvin Barnett works on his top-end speed technique.

Tommie Hill (Oakland Raiders) develops power with the use of power cleans.

Guy Miller uses single-arm shoulder press lingers to develop flexibility and strength.

on season-ending reserve. Eight months post-cervical fusion, Scaife signed with the New England Patriots.

Players with season-ending injuries often wind up spending their season with Landow.

Among Landow's many features as a performance coach, extending an athlete's career may be his specialty. Two examples are offensive tackle Erik Pears and defensive lineman Trevor Pryce.

Few players have experienced the kind of bummed-to-beaming swing that can match the professional career of offensive tackle Erik Pears. Undrafted out of Colorado State, Pears was one of the last to play in the now defunct NFL Europe league. He spent 2005 on the Broncos' practice squad, became a starter almost by default in 2006–2007, didn't play a game in 2008, became a part-time starter for the Oakland Raiders in 2009, then was cut multiple times in 2010—three times by the Raiders, once by Jacksonville.

It got so bad for Pears in 2010, he wound up playing two games for the Omaha Nighthawks in the United Football League.

After 2010, Pears worked out with Landow's group throughout the lockout.

"He was so fast, so athletic, but in Oakland he got too big," Landow said. "We worked on returning him to the type of agility he had, his knee bend. We worked a lot on his explosive first steps."

Pears became a sixteen-game starter for the Buffalo Bills in 2011. By November, the Bills were so pleased with Pears, who was playing at a Pro Bowl level, they gave him a three-year, $9.3-million extension.

Trevor Pryce was arguably the Broncos' best defensive lineman from his second season of 1998 until he was unceremoniously released following a fine 2005 season in which he helped Denver to the AFC championship game.

The Broncos, though, were concerned about Pryce's chronic back troubles. He quickly signed with the Baltimore Ravens, who traditionally had the league's most feared defense—because the league's most feared player, Ray Lewis, was their middle line-backer.

The reality of his football mortality sent Pryce to Landow that off-season for a regular routine of football-related workouts. In 2006, Pryce's first year with the Ravens, he tied for fifth in the league with thirteen sacks. Pryce played five more seasons after the Broncos essentially told him he was finished.

That second career was launched from the platform of Landow's workouts. Players know this is not an exaggeration.

"He trained me in a way that was functional to what I do to make a living," Dreessen said. "As far as movement. He gets you strong in your movement, he gets you fast with your movement, and he increases your flexibility. And he has such a positive attitude. He tells you what you need to do over the course of the weekend, nutrition-wise, not drinking, not partying."

Landow's advice helped return Dreessen to the NFL and, eventually, to his hometown team. As the Broncos went off to training camp without him, Landow was still working with NFL players such as Scaife, former Broncos Karl Paymah and Demetrin Veal, and several other players who were trying to get back in the league.

Landow did feel, more than ever before, a small sense of ownership in the Broncos. Rightly so. When you train these players—and again, between twenty-five and thirty-five players participated in the Broncos players-only workouts that ran from early May to late July—it's not unusual for any coach to refer to the group as "my players."

Landow is a coach. There are coaches who instruct linemen on how to block. They are called offensive line coaches. There are coaches who coordinate the entire defense. They are called defensive coordinators. And there are coaches who instruct players on how to warm up their bodies, strengthen them, enhance their quick-twitch muscles, isolate the technique of a proper first step, running form, blocking and tackling form, and instill proper injury prevention and recovery methods.

They are called sports performance coaches.

Thanks in no small part to Landow's coaching, so many Broncos players were more ready than ever for Broncos training camp.

"One thing I think he does better than others—for me, I'm a visual learner," said Broncos backup quarterback Brady Quinn. "So when I see things, it helps me learn. And he is athletic enough to actually demonstrate. He is so good at what he does, it helps you understand what you should look like while doing the drills."

There are player-coaches. In Landow's field of expertise, he's a good enough athlete that he could be considered a performer-coach instead of a performance coach. He doesn't just order his athletes to high step through the ladders. He shows them first.

As the Broncos went off to Dove Valley, Quinn and Tim Tebow would always come back. The two backup quarterbacks. Upon further thought, it makes sense. Backup quarterbacks, more than any other position on the team, can build up the most rust in their performance. They do not stay sharp by running down the field on special teams to tackle the returner or block for the returner, as backup linebackers and receivers will. They do not mix it up with the others during padded practices.

Yet, at no other position is it more imperative to be ready when called up than the backup quarterback. For all the sedentary tasks that come with his role as backup, no one on the team, no one among the 75,000 watching from the stands, not one of the millions watching at home, would excuse a poor performance when he's called upon in an emergency.

If the starting quarterback gets crushed in the second quarter and the team is behind 10–7, it doesn't matter if the backup quarterback has been asked to do little more than hold a clipboard the previous six weeks. It's the backup quarterback's job to get in there and win the game. That's all. Nothing less is expected.

And so as training camp was winding down and the season

was about to begin, Quinn and Tebow would come in on Tuesdays to work out with Landow. At different times. After working out together the other six days of the week, after spending all that time together in meetings and the weight room and practice field, it helps for all players to get away from each other on their Tuesdays off.

Besides, what good would Tebow's hour be with Landow if he had to share instruction with Quinn? And Landow's instruction went beyond biomotor skills.

He knew a little bit about a quarterback's passing mechanics. The dropback. The setup with the feet. The throwing position. The release and delivery.

Something else Quinn and Tebow had in common: Neither is a textbook-type learner. Quinn learns when he sees. Tebow is dyslexic. He learns by doing. In psychology terms, Tebow is considered a kinesthetic learner.

"Rather than being auditory or visual, kinesthetic is learning by doing," Tebow said. "So if you say, 'Let's figure out how to work this TV . . .' Well, if you just tell me: 'Hit this, this and this,' I won't remember it as well. But if I go through it and do it, then I'll have it."

When Tebow talks to youths—and besides playing football, there is nothing else he'd rather be doing—he leaves them believing dyslexia is more a learning skill than a disability.

"I don't think it's a handicap at all for me," he said. "It's just about processing differently. It's something that interests me, because kids learn so much differently. There's not a cookie-cutter way of, 'Hey, this is how it is and based on these tests, this is your intelligence level.' No, that's silly. Some kids are brilliant in different ways. I feel bad when kids can't test well; they're not looked at as smart."

Underrated in Landow's ability to train elite athletes is that he trains all kinds. Even after Tebow became the Broncos' starting quarterback, he continued to work out weekly with Landow. He continued to call Landow almost daily for the next day's workout, for advice, for consultation. For friendship. Tim Tebow, whose extreme dedication to his craft and body made him one of the last to turn it over to Landow, had grown to trust the performance coach. Trust him with every fiber in his body.

Why wouldn't he? When Tebow was called upon to replace Kyle Orton at halftime of the Broncos' fifth game against the rival San Diego Chargers on October 9, the lefty-throwing quarterback proved he was ready.

His spectacular fourth-quarter comeback bid, even if it fell short when his final Hail Mary to the end zone was knocked down, proved he deserved to start.

CHAPTER 10

A Championship Season While Everyone Was Watching

FTER THE LOCKOUT, and all the Broncos players returned to training camp, the preseason, and regular season with the team's coaching staff, Loren Landow felt fortunate he didn't have to go cold turkey without his favorite group of players.

Brady Quinn and Tim Tebow continued on with regular, one-on-one workouts with Landow. As backup quarterbacks, Quinn and Tebow didn't get the number of reps in practice they needed to stay sharp. The way it works with most NFL teams, including the Broncos, is that the starting quarterback, in this case Kyle Orton, gets all the reps with the first-team offense.

The second- and third-stringers work with the second-string and third-string offense. And the backups don't get nearly the practice that the first team does.

Once the season starts, almost all practice reps go to the first team. There's a game to play Sunday and only so much time to prepare. The backups are expected to be ready, anyway. And so Quinn and Tebow felt they needed to get in some work outside the Broncos' facility to stay sharp.

That's where Landow could help.

For the most part, Tebow spent Sundays observing from the sidelines, encouraging his teammates but also wishing he could contribute. With patience the season would come to him.

Tebow came off the bench in the second half against the San Diego Chargers with the Broncos down, 23–10. It was game 5 of the regular season, October 9, in front of the Broncos' home fans at Sports Authority Field at Mile High, and Tebow put on an exhilarating, fourth-quarter comeback that nearly pulled out a victory.

Tebow had a 12-yard touchdown run and 28-yard touchdown pass in back-to-back, late drives; then, he had two long pass completions in his abbreviated final drive of the game.

A Hail Mary pass, thrown after Tebow scrambled for twelve seconds as timed by Associated Press writer Pat Graham, fell incomplete to end the game. But not two seconds later, even though the Broncos had just lost 29–24 to the AFC West rival Chargers, the home crowd chanted: "Te-bow! Te-bow!"

Following a bye week, the Broncos led by Tebow rallied from a 15–0 deficit to defeat the Dolphins at Miami. It was the first time in NFL history a team had overcome a 15-point deficit with less than three minutes remaining in the game.

This comeback became the start of what became commonly known around the NFL as Tebow Time. If there were a definition of Tebow Time, it would be this: Team is down. Clock is winding down. All seems lost. And, then, with a lot of help from his friends—whether special teams recovering an onside kick; the defense forcing a running back out of bounds, saving valuable final seconds; tight end Daniel Fells making a spectacular diving catch down the middle of the field; or a defensive standout such as Elvis Dumervil coming up with a drive-stopping sack at the most crucial time—Tebow makes a run or pass or play to help pull out a victory.

The week after the exhilarating Dolphins' game, the Broncos

were humbled by the red-hot Detroit Lions, who seemed to take out years of frustration on many opponents in 2011.

The Lions put a licking on the Broncos, 45–10. Especially embarrassing for the Broncos was that the game was played in front of their home crowd at Sports Authority Field.

At this point, it didn't seem to matter whether Orton or Tebow was the quarterback. The Broncos were 2–5 and seemingly going nowhere.

Then the Broncos got an enormous boost from their coaching staff. Head coach John Fox wanted his offense to better take advantage of Tebow's unique skill set. What makes Tebow unique? By NFL standards, it's his dual-threat option of pass and run. Most NFL quarterbacks are only dangerous with the arm.

Dual-threat option. Dual-threat option. You can almost hear those words echoing in Fox's brain.

He decided to implement a variation of the spread—read option—Tebow used so effectively during his Heisman Trophy-winning career at the University of Florida in the Broncos' offense.

Fox had offensive coordinator Mike McCoy and quarterbacks coach Adam Gase teach the read option to the rest of the offense during meetings, practice, and walk-throughs.

Presto change-o! In their first game with the read option, Tebow, running back Willis McGahee, the offensive line, and the receivers blocking downfield both befuddled and steamrolled the Raiders in Oakland for a 38–24 win.

The Broncos' rushing totals looked more like they were stolen from an Air Force Falcons' game against a weak Western Athletic Conference opponent. On thirty-nine carries, the Broncos amassed a staggering 299 yards rushing for 7.7 yards per carry.

And it would have been an even 300 yards except the statisticians gave Tebow –1 yard on his game-ending kneel down from what is known as the Victory Formation.

McGahee (163) and Tebow (118) each rushed for more than one hundred yards. The running attack also opened up explosive passing plays for Tebow. He wound up throwing touchdown passes of 27 yards to Eric Decker and 29 yards to Eddie Royal.

After the win against the Raiders, the buzz around the NFL wasn't so much about Tebow as about the read option. The *Denver Post* wrote stories explaining the read option in detail. ESPN would use film or Telestrators to show the "read" Tebow had to make in the read option.

Not only had the Broncos defeated the Raiders; they were now 2–0 on the road against AFC opponents since Tebow became the starting quarterback. Those wins against AFC teams became significant at season's end as they helped the Broncos win tiebreakers against Oakland and San Diego.

After whipping the Raiders on November 6, Tebow led the Broncos to a 17–10 win at Kansas City on November 13. It was Tebow's 56-yard touchdown pass to Eric Decker midway through the fourth quarter that provided the margin of victory.

The Broncos ran the ball a Woody Hayes-like fifty-five times against the Chiefs, for 244 yards, while Tebow completed only two of eight passes.

This was a game where a journeyman running back named Lance Ball became a Broncos' workhorse. During the lockout, Ball probably would have won the skill position attendance award at Camp Dawkins, had such an award been given.

Ball is an inspirational story of perseverance and resiliency. He was not drafted out of the University of Maryland in 2008. He signed on with the St. Louis Rams as an undrafted free agent. Among the last cuts in his rookie training camp, Ball was re-signed to the Rams' practice squad on September 1, 2008, but was waived before month's end.

He then signed on with the Indianapolis Colts' practice squad. And on Ball would bounce—from the Colts' practice squad, to the Tennessee Titans' practice squad, to the Broncos' practice squad, and finally during the 2010 season, Ball made the Broncos' active, 53-man roster.

He had been cut five times by four teams, including once by the Broncos in September of 2009.

He wasn't flashy, which is why he had trouble sticking in the first place, but he was remarkably consistent, so that when he did get his opportunity, he stuck.

Said Landow: "When the opportunity of a lifetime presents itself, you have to act within the lifetime of the opportunity."

When McGahee went down with a leg pull, and then backup Knowshon Moreno suffered an unfortunate ACL tear that ended his season, Lance Ball was thrust within the lifetime of his opportunity.

Ball got not one carry, or two, or five carries. He got thirty. A thirty-carry game.

For a guy who had thirteen carries in three years, Ball did not feel overly beat up for having a career-high thirty carries in one game. After the game, Ball made a statement that was music to his summer performance coach's ears:

"It felt good," Ball said. "It didn't even feel like thirty carries."

Ball not only worked out regularly with the Landow-supervised Broncos workouts during the lockout summer of 2011, he would help load the ice coolers into the vehicle of camp organizer Judianne Atencio.

All that hard work during the summer? Those thirty carries Sunday against the Chiefs were worth every drop of perspiration.

"The guy is hungry," said Eric Studesville, the Broncos' running backs coach. "He knows the window of opportunity for him might be small, and you've got to be ready for it when it's there."

The Broncos were 3–1 with Tebow as their starting quarterback. More impressively, they were 3–0 on the road.

As the football nation adjusted to Tebow's unique style of play, he picked up a convert in New York Jets' coach Rex Ryan when the Broncos played a Thursday night, prime-time game on November 17.

Ryan seemed to have an effective defensive game plan for stopping Tebow until 5 minutes, 54 seconds remained in the game. The Broncos were backed up on their own 4½-yard line, and they were down 13–10.

The only reason the Broncos were within one score was because punter Britton Colquitt continually left the Jets with poor starting field position.

On the first play of that series, Tebow threw a screen pass to Eddie Royal, who was nearly tackled in the end zone for a safety. Had Royal been tackled there, the 2-point safety would have put the Broncos further behind at 15–10. They would have had to free-kick the ball back to the Jets. In turn, the Jets could have chewed up more clock.

All factors that most likely would have led to defeat. The Broncos' record would have fallen to 4–6, and they would have been all but eliminated from the play-offs. See how thin the margin of success is to each team in each NFL season?

The Camp Dawkins workouts during the summer may have given the Broncos no more than a 1-percent advantage over any particular opponent during the 2011 season. But with the margin between success and failure so slim, who knows? The difference might have been one more workout, one more rep, one more word of instruction, one more dreaded run at Red Rocks.

On that final, 95-yard, game-winning drive against the Jets, Tebow had back-to-back long runs where he broke pass-rush containment, then cut in smoothly against a would-be tackler. The cut-in gained him an additional six to eight yards each time.

Actually, on the second run, it wasn't Tebow avoiding a tackle but Jets star cornerback Darrelle Revis avoiding Tebow. The point is, the quarterback ran more like an elusive tailback than a bulldozing fullback.

In finishing off the drive, Tebow scrambled away from a safety blitz pass rush and sprinted in for a 20-yard touchdown with 58 seconds remaining.

The crowd shook the rivets at Sports Authority Field. A national cable audience was beginning to believe that the Tebow-led Broncos were a legitimate play-off contender.

The Broncos had three wins in a row and a 4–1 record with Tebow as the starter. The run had evened the Broncos' record to 5–5, one game behind the AFC West-leading Oakland Raiders.

Tebow was captivating not only a football nation, but the nation, period. Not only were the Broncos receiving extensive coverage from ESPN and the NFL Network; Tebow and the Broncos were featured on CNN, the *Today Show*, Jay Leno, David Letterman, and the nightly network news shows.

The Broncos had gone from 1–4 to the talk of the country.

After the win against the Jets, Landow made a significant adjustment to Tebow's training. Their relationship had grown. With each session, Tebow trusted Landow more to work on his body. And with each session, Landow understood better how to adjust the workouts so that Tebow could continue to maximize his game-day performance.

"Training with Loren was a great mixture of working hard and specifically working on the things I needed most," Tebow said.

As the Broncos' season was evolving with their new quarterback, two things became common in Tebow's games: One, as a rare, dual-threat athlete, he carried the ball more than most quarterbacks. And two, Tebow was remarkable in the clutch. In the fourth quarter, with the outcome in doubt, when hearts would race and the energy was at its highest, Tebow was at his best.

He thrived in these situations.

But these two characteristics that were unique to Tebow also required some extra preparation. Landow started to implement a workout that is more common with his Mixed Martial Arts (MMA) athletes. It's not quite as widely known that Landow trains some of the best Ultimate Fight Championship (UFC) fighters in the world: Brendan Schaub, Nate Marquardt, Shane Carwin, Eliot Marshall, and Jared Hammon, to name a few.

UFC fighters are some of the best-conditioned athletes in the world. And these MMA fighters benefit from an interval strategy called Tabata.

Developed by Izumi Tabata, the main objective is to delay the onset of the lactate threshold. It was after the Jets' game that Tabata became part of Tebow's workouts. Tebow and Tabata. Tabata and Tebow.

Using a VersaClimber, a lean machine that's a tad more dialed up in terms of intensity than a StairMaster, Tebow would go through 20-second intervals of work followed by 10 seconds off. Then 20 seconds more of churning, followed by 10 seconds off.

Seven rounds of 3:30 total minutes of undulated workload and rest.

There was one more tweak Landow added to Tebow's Tabata workout. Not only did Tebow have to be physically able to lead his team on final-minute, win-or-else drives, he had to communicate effectively with his ten offensive teammates.

Tebow loves to lead through encouragement: "Way to pick up the blitz, J.D.!" "Thanks for saving my backside, Kupe!" "Nice catch, Deck!"

And then there is the quarterback's responsibility of calling the plays in the huddle. Ever trying calling a play that has a bunch of letters and numbers and formations after breaking two tackles and cutting in and out for a 20-yard gain? It's not easy.

So Landow had Tebow wear a mouthpiece while working through his Tabata intervals. Not only wear a mouthpiece during Tabata, but Landow would have Tebow carry on a conversation as he was working.

Said Landow: "What I was trying to do was calm his breathing pattern down while exercising so Tim could clearly communicate. Tim is a phenomenal athlete with a rare blend of ability, work ethic, and a never-ending desire to improve."

Better believe Landow didn't add Tabata, didn't add Tabata with the mouthpiece, didn't add Tabata with the mouthpiece and conversation, without discussing his methods with Tebow.

"Tim wants to know the hows and whys to every workout and every exercise," Landow said.

"He used a very scientific approach to our workouts and explained why we were doing each individual exercise in a manner that made sense to me," Tebow said. "Most importantly, there were noticeable improvements in my overall stamina and conditioning, which significantly helped me throughout the season."

After the Jets' game, the Broncos would play game 11 of their season at San Diego, in a rematch against the Chargers. Tebow posted an impressive 95.4 passer rating in a 16–13 overtime win.

Tebow was 5–1 as a starter, 4–0 on the road overall, and 3–0 on the road against AFC West opponents. To be sure, it wasn't just Tebow. The offensive line, 60 percent of whom were regular participants of Camp Dawkins during the lockout, opened up enough gaping holes for Tebow and tailback Willis McGahee to push the Broncos to the number one rushing team in the NFL.

And as the winning scores indicate—18–15 in overtime against Miami, 17–10 against Kansas City, 17–13 against the Jets, 16–13 in overtime against the Chargers—the defense was at times sensational while keeping the game close enough so Tebow could perform his magic late.

There was enough credit to go around, but it probably wasn't a coincidence that before Tebow got his chance to lead, the Broncos were last in the AFC West with a 1–4 record, and now they were second with a 6–5 mark, just one game behind first-place Oakland.

The Broncos moved into a first-place tie the next week by rallying from behind to beat the Vikings in Minnesota, 35–32. Tebow had an explosive passing day, completing 10 of 15 passes but for 202 yards, two touchdowns, no interceptions, and a robust 149.3 passer rating.

The Broncos were behind 15–7 at halftime, with their only touchdown coming on an interception return by linebacker Mario Haggan.

It was in the second half that Tebow and the Broncos' offense found its rhythm. Tebow would throw touchdown passes of 21 and 41 yards to Demaryius Thomas. He completed only six of eight passes in the second half for 178 Viking-damaging yards.

"I mean, the dude lit us up," said Vikings star defensive end Jared Allen.

It was the longer touchdown pass to Thomas that perhaps became the most symbolic play of what Tebow is all about. First,Tebow escaped what seemed to be a certain sack and scrambled left. He kept his eyes downfield waiting for a receiver to come open.

Meanwhile, Vikings linebacker Erin Henderson was closing in. Keep in mind, Henderson is not a 185-pound cornerback. He does not wear #25. Henderson wears #50. He is 6-foot-3, 244 pounds.

Tebow swatted him away with a stiff-arm. A split second later, Tebow drilled a pass down the seam to Thomas, who had worked himself open. Thomas took it in from there.

In one play, Tebow showed the athleticism of a tailback, the strength of a linebacker, the arm of a quarterback.

The Broncos were now working on a five-game winning streak. They were 6–1 with Tebow as their starter, 7–5 overall. From 1–4, the Broncos were tied with the slumping Raiders for the AFC West lead.

The Broncos would have one more regular-season win in him.

It was against the Bears on December 11. The teams went into their halftime locker rooms tied, 0–0.

It didn't get much better for the Broncos in the second half. They were down 10–0 with less than 2:15 remaining, when again Tebow performed a miraculous comeback, throwing a 10-yard touchdown pass to Demaryius Thomas, and then Prater kicked a 59-yard field goal with three seconds remaining to tie it.

Prater booted another long-distance field goal in overtime, this time from 51 yards, and the Broncos had their sixth consecutive win.

Yes, the Broncos received some remarkably good fortune. First, after Tebow's touchdown pass to Demaryius Thomas pulled the Broncos to 10–7, the Bears got the ball back with only 2:08 remaining.

Following the two minutes remaining, the Broncos got a break when Bears running back Marion Barber III ran out of bounds, stopping the clock. Had he stayed in bounds, the Broncos would have received the ball back with about 20 seconds remaining. Instead, the Broncos got it back with 53 seconds left. Just enough time for Tebow to complete passes of 9 and 11 yards, before he connected with Matt Willis for another 19 yards. The ball was moved to the Bears' 41. Prater boomed it from there, and Prater did it again in overtime. The Broncos were an incredible 7–1 with Tebow as a starter.

To show how much the Broncos became a resilient collection of clutch performers, in three of those seven wins, the Broncos never led until there was 0:00 left on the clock. Talk about playing to the end. The 2011 Broncos were good to the sixtieth minute.

In a much-publicized game against Tom Brady and the mighty New England Patriots, Tebow played well, leading the Broncos to an early 16–7 lead. He rushed for 93 yards on just twelve carries in that game and passed for 194 yards on just eleven completions.

Yet, the Broncos suffered three turnovers in the second quarter and never recovered. The Pats took the lead and won, 41–23.

The winning streak was snapped at six, but as it turned out, the Broncos had already clinched the AFC West title with their win against the Chicago Bears.

For the first time in six years, the Broncos were back in the play-offs. However, their first-round opponent was the traditionally rough, tough Pittsburgh Steelers.

When the 2011 regular season had finished, the Steelers had the number one-rated defense. They had tremendous defensive stars such as Troy Polamalu and James Harrison.

Front-office boss John Elway, the greatest quarterback in Broncos' history, went public with his advice to Tebow. Elway told *Denver Post* columnist Woody Paige he wanted his young quarterback to "pull the trigger."

Tebow didn't pull the trigger. He launched bombs throughout Sports Authority Field. Early in the second quarter, he tossed a gorgeous 51-yard completion to Demaryius Thomas. One play later, Tebow threw a perfect 30-yard touchdown pass to Eddie Royal.

Tebow hit Thomas again on the next possession for a 58-yard gain, then ran it in for an 8-yard touchdown. The Broncos were 20–6 at halftime.

Although the Steelers rallied to tie the game, 23–23, Tebow needed just one play in overtime to win it.

With the Tebow to Thomas 80-yard touchdown connection, Colorado erupted in a delirious celebration.

Tebow finished the game with a career-best 316 passing yards, the two touchdown passes, and a touchdown run. He is a true double threat.

The Broncos had not only won the AFC West, they had won a play-off game for the first time since the 2005 season, and for only the second time since John Elway as quarterback led the

Joe Mays leads the group in a dynamic flexibility exercise, lateral A skips. Eric Decker, Cassius Vaughn, Chris Gronkowski, Lance Ball, Brian Dawkins, Ben Garland, Chris Clark, Jeff Byers, J. D. Walton, and Zane Beadles participate.

Broncos to their second consecutive Super Bowl in the 1998 season.

Put another way, the 2011 Broncos had one of their top two seasons of the past thirteen years. And to think, it all started during the NFL lockout in the summer, when Brian Dawkins gathered a group of his Broncos teammates to work out under the direction of sports performance coach Loren Landow, when nobody was watching.

Upper-Body Strength Exercises

Upper-body strength push-up, modified (beginner). Alignment from ear to ankle. Hands slightly wider than shoulders. Slowly lower the chest toward the bar with control and with core braced. As the elbows get to the plane of the back, push into the bar with your hands and return back to the top position. Repeat for the desired reps without compromising technique.

Upper-body strength push (intermediate). Alignment from ear to ankle. Hands roughly shoulder width and elbows 45 degrees from shoulder and back. Slowly lower the chest toward the ground with control and with core braced. As the elbows get to the plane of the back, push into the ground with your hands and return back to the start position. Repeat for the desired reps without compromising technique.

Upper-body strength push (advanced). Alignment from ear to ankle with stable medicine ball under chest. Hands roughly shoulder width and elbows 45 degrees from shoulder and back. Slowly lower chest toward the ball, and once you have slightly touched it, explosively push through the hands into the ground and create as much separation from the floor. With arms slightly bent (5 degrees), stick with both hand on the medicine ball while keeping the core braced. Repeat for the desired reps without compromising technique.

Upper-body strength pull, modified (beginner) TRX, barbell. Alignment from ear to ankle holding with a neutral grip. Shoulders down and back, pull the elbows through the plane of the back while maintaining an extended spinal position with core braced. Slowly extend the arms and lower the back to the starting position with a slight bend in the elbows. Repeat for the desired reps without compromising technique.

Upper-body strength pull, horizontal (intermediate). Body parallel to the ground, feet elevated 8–10". Alignment from ear to ankle, core braced. Shoulders down and back, pulling the elbows through the plane of the back while maintaining an extended spinal position with core braced. Slowly extend the arms and lower the back to the starting position with arms extended. Repeat for the desired reps without compromising technique.

Upper-body strength pull, horizontal (advanced). Body parallel to the ground, feet on a bench. Alignment from ear to ankle, core braced. Shoulders down and back, pulling the elbows through the plane of the back while maintaining extended spinal position and keeping the core braced. Push heels into bench and pull the torso toward the feet and squeeze the hamstrings. Fully extend the legs and lower the back to the starting position while keeping the core braced. Repeat for the desired reps without compromising technique.

Upper-body strength pull, horizontal (advanced). Continued.

Postscript

FOR MANY PEOPLE, it's not how long you live but that you are healthy for as long as you live.

It's the same with football, only the lives are shorter.

Brian Dawkins, the leader of the Broncos during the lockout of 2011 and for three years in the locker room, earned his ninth Pro Bowl berth in his sixteenth NFL season. He played in 70.2 percent of the Broncos' defensive snaps at thirty-eight years of age, even though he essentially missed the final three regular-season games and two play-off games because of an ill-timed pinched nerve in his neck. The nine Pro Bowls tied for the second-most all-time among NFL safeties.

Dawkins announced his retirement in April 2012, not because of his neck injury—that had completely healed—but, in large part, because he had played at a high level for most of his final season.

"This is going to sound real crazy, but it's the fact that I could play another year that led me to the belief that I should go ahead and stop now," Dawkins said.

Dawkins, in his three years with the Broncos, may not have been quite the dynamic and dominant player he was during his first thirteen seasons with the Philadelphia Eagles.

He was a very good player with the Broncos, though, and his final season was nothing less than a lesson in leadership and passion for the game. Not only did Dawkins organize the Broncos' players-only workouts under the direction of sports performance coach Loren Landow, the safety accepted a severe pay cut from

$6 million to $2 million so he could help push the team in the right direction before he bowed out.

Remember, the Broncos were a 4–12 team entering the lockout. Thanks in part to Camp Dawkins, the Broncos won the AFC West title and a play-off game for the first time in six years.

"I think it [Camp Dawkins] played 'a' role," Dawkins said. "I don't know if it played an important role or whatever, but it did play a role."

One of the most regular participants in Camp Dawkins, and then later when it became Camp Landow, was Broncos middle linebacker Joe Mays. To think that the Broncos had selected Nate Irving in the third round of the 2011 draft essentially to take Mays's place.

But after Mays's fine season in 2011, he became a free agent and drew serious enough interest from New Orleans and Indianapolis that the Broncos re-signed him to a three-year, $12-million contract.

Chris Kuper had surgery to remove a bothersome pin in his leg in March 2012, and it did wonders for his recovery; the Broncos' right guard was hopeful of lining up with the first-team offense in time for the final minicamp in mid-June.

And, yes, unlike 2011, there was an off-season conditioning program, OTAs, and a minicamp for the Broncos in 2012.

Brady Quinn never did take a snap in his two seasons with the Broncos. He became a free agent after the 2011 season and, though the Broncos were hopeful of bringing him back, Quinn decided to change his luck. He signed a one-year contract with the Kansas City Chiefs, where he will back up not Peyton Manning but Matt Cassel. In time, Quinn may finally get his chance to regain a starting position, in Kansas City.

Peyton Manning, not Tim Tebow, is the Broncos' starting quarterback for 2012. In a decision that many applauded, but not all, Broncos bosses John Elway and John Fox, with owner Pat Bowlen's blessing, decided to pursue Manning in free agency.

Manning was about to turn thirty-six, and he had missed the entire 2011 season with a neck injury. But he is also one of the greatest quarterbacks in NFL history, and his career was not finished.

The Broncos out-recruited at least nine other teams who were bidding for Manning and signed the league's four-time MVP to a five-year, $96-million contract.

Manning's signing was met with mixed reaction in Denver. Everyone acknowledged that he is great. But what Tebow did for the Broncos in 2011 was a story for the ages.

To Manning's credit, he was extremely respectful of what Tebow had done for the Broncos in 2011.

"What an awesome year he had this year," Manning said at his introductory press conference March 20. "If other opportunities present themselves for him, I'm going to wish him the best. He's going to be a great player wherever he is."

Manning's arrival left the Broncos' brass believing they had no choice but to trade away Tebow. The quarterback was so popular, such a point of discussion, that the team did not want Manning to deal with any potential distraction.

Tebow was the player the Broncos would love to have kept. It was Tebowmania that Elway and Fox wanted to discard. The day after Manning was introduced as the Broncos' new quarterback, the man he replaced—the man who led the Broncos from 1–4 to the play-offs in 2011—was traded to the New York Jets.

Tebow's departure meant there would be no quarterback controversy in Denver. Tebow's arrival in New York meant there would be a new quarterback with the Jets, where the incumbent quarterback is Mark Sanchez.

"I would never bet against Tim Tebow," Loren Landow said. "Never!"

Index

acceleration: burst, *62*; Larsen and Mays and, 75; A runs, *123*; transition to, 76, *104*

acceleration progression drills: overview about, 99; partner-resisted A run, *103*; partner-resisted march, *102*; wall drills, *100*, *101*

activation exercises, 56

Adams, Rileigh, 128

adaptation, 55–56

adenosine triphosphate phospho-creatine (ATP-PC) energy system, 98

AFC. *See* American Football Conference play-off game

Agyei, Augustine, 128

Allen, Jared, 170

Allen, Mike, 52

American Football Conference (AFC) play-off game: details, 172; odds, 3; Tebow and Thomas, Demaryius, touchdown at, 1, 25–26

Anderson, Derek, 114

ankle mobility, 74

anti-rotational exercises: kneeling cable-chop, *23*; sandbell power rotations, *24*; seated alternate leg raise, *20*; seated partner rhythmic stability, *21*; standing partner anti-rotation stability, *22*

asthma, 41

Atencio, Judianne, *143*, 144; clients of, 82; Landow's proposal and, 30–32; media day organized by, 81–82; as public relations expert, 32; role of, 4

ATP-PC. *See* adenosine triphosphate phospho-creatine energy system

Ayers, Robert, 129, *142*; knee injury of, 76

Bailey, Champ, 138

Ball, Lance, *127*, 129, *173*; as explosive, 76; opportunity for, 165; perseverance of, 164–65; regular attendance of, 126

Baltimore Ravens, 156–57

Bannan, Justin, 150

Barber, Marion, III, 171

barefoot cooldown, 63

barefoot series: 1-count hop stick, *117*; 2-count hop stick, *118*; 3-count hop stick, *119*; 5-count hop stick, *120*; purpose of, 116–17

Barnett, Alvin, *153*

Beadles, Zane, 129, 142, *173*; knee bend and, 74; Sports Xcel and, 51

Bears. *See* Chicago Bears

Bengals. *See* Cincinnati Bengals

Bills. *See* Buffalo Bills

Bing, Brandon, 134

biomotor abilities, 152

bodybuilding, 44–45

Solder, Nate, 150, *151*

Sosa, Sammy, 47

South Suburban Sports Dome, 9

Sports Xcel, 51

squats: with asymmetrical load, *59*; beginner, *57*; squat jumps, *60*; weighted, *58*

stability series: anti-rotational exercises, *20–24*; lateral, *14–16*; lateral plank, *15*; lateral plank elevated, *15*; lateral plank elevated with leg lift, *13*; lateral plank kneeling, *14*; plank, *12*; plank with hip hike, *12*; plank with leg raise, *13*; posterior stability, *16–19*

standing partner anti-rotation stability, *22*

Steadman Hawkins Clinic, 2, 52

Steelers. *See* Pittsburgh Steelers

straight-leg series: prone abduction, *73*; side-lying abduction, *71*; side-lying adduction, *72*; supine high kick, *70*

strength and conditioning position, Broncos, 64

stretch-shortening reflex, 9

Studdard, Kasey, 150

Studesville, Eric, 115, 165

Sumner, Blaine, 150

supine high kick, *70*

Sylvan Learning Center, 43–44

Tabata, Izumi, 168

Tanaka, Chris, 87

Taylor, Dain, 122

Taylor, Ike, 25, 26

Tebow, Tim: Bears game and, 171; combined sessions and, 110; communication and, 168–69; criticism of, 77, 85; dyslexia and, 159; final-quarter comebacks of, 6–7; as instinctual, 7; Jets game and, 166; joining Camp Dawkins, 7–8; Landow earning trust of, 8; Landow's opening conversation with, 3; McDaniels and, 115; media day absence of, 84; *Through My Eyes* by, 84; one-on-one training and, 159–61, 167–69; Patriots game and, 171–72; playoff overtime touchdown and, 1, 25–26; promotion of, 139–40; rushing yards of, 163; as starting quarterback, 140–41; Steelers game and, 172; as superstar, 83; Tabata training and, 168; on team togetherness, 10; trading of, 183; Vikings game and, 169–70; work ethic of, 2, 8–9

Tebowmania, 139

Tebow Time, 162

Tennessee Titans, 138–39, 152

Testaverde, Vinny, 145

Texans. *See* Houston Texans

Thomas, Demaryius, 171, 172; Achilles surgery and, 125; injury to, 134; playoff overtime touchdown and, 1, 25–26; Vikings game and, 170

Thomas, Julius, 126; athleticism of, 75–76; initiative of, 77

Thomas, Marcus, 134, 137

3-count hop stick, *119*

300 shuttle, *97*

Through My Eyes (Tebow), 84

tight end, 147

Titans. *See* Tennessee Titans

transfer of forces, 11, 25

2-count hop stick, *118*

two-minute drill: Quinn, Brady, and, 113–14, 130–31; success of, 113

2011 Broncos season. *See* Denver Broncos' 2011 season